Ancient Aramaic and Hebrew Letters

Writings from the Ancient World
Society of Biblical Literature

Burke O. Long, General Editor

Associate Editors

Gary Beckman
Jo Ann Hackett
Edmund Meltzer
Patrick Miller, Jr.
William Murnane
David Owen
Martha Roth
Raymond Westbrook

Volume 4
Ancient Aramaic and Hebrew Letters
by James M. Lindenberger
Edited by Kent Harold Richards

Ancient Aramaic and Hebrew Letters

by
James M. Lindenberger

Edited by
Kent Harold Richards

Scholars Press
Atlanta, Georgia

The Society of Biblical Literature gratefully acknowledges a grant
from the National Endowment for the Humanities to underwrite
certain editorial and research expenses of the Writings from
the Ancient World series. Published results and interpretations
do not necessarily represent the view of the Endowment.

Library of Congress Cataloging-in-Publication Data

Ancient Aramaic and Hebrew Letters / [compiled] by James M.
  Lindenberger ; edited by Kent Harold Richards.
      p.   cm. — (Writings from the ancient world ; no. 04)
  Includes bibliographical references and index.
  ISBN 1-55540-839-7 (cloth). — ISBN 1-55540-840-0 (pbk.)
    1. Aramaic letters.   2. Aramaic letters—Translations into
English   3. Hebrew letters.   4. Hebrew letters—Translations into
English.   5. Middle East—History—To 622—Sources.
  I. Lindenberger, James M.   II. Richards, Kent Harold, 1939–
  III. Series.
  PJ5208.A2A54   1993
  492′.2—dc20   93-6657
                                                          CIP

Printed in the United States of America
on acid-free paper.

Contents

Series Editor's Foreword

Writings from the Ancient World (WAW) presents up-to-date, reliable, and felicitous English translations of important documents from the ancient Near East. Covering the period from the beginning of Sumerian civilization to the age of Alexander, WAW tries to meet research needs of specialists while contributing to general education and cultural awareness.

Translators and editors have kept in mind a broad audience that includes, among others, scholars in the humanities for whom convenient access to new and reliable translations will aid comparative work; general readers, educators, and students for whom these materials may help increase awareness of our cultural roots in preclassical civilizations; specialists in particular cultures of the ancient world who may not control the languages of neighboring societies.

The editors envision that over time the series will include collections of myths, epics, poetry, and law codes; historical and diplomatic materials such as treaties and commemorative inscriptions; and letters and commercial documents. Other volumes will offer translations of hymns, prayers, rituals, and other documents of religious practice. The aim is to provide a representative, rather than exhaustive, sample of writings that broadly represent the cultural remains of various ancient civilizations.

The preparation of this volume was supported in part by a generous grant from the Division of Research Programs of the National Endowment for the Humanities. The Society of Biblical Literature also provided significant financial and administrative support. In addition, all scholars involved in preparing this volume received financial and clerical assistance from their respective institutions. Were it not for these expressions of confidence in our intentions, the arduous tasks of preparation, translation, editing, and publication—indeed, planning for the series itself—simply would not have been undertaken.

James Lindenberger prepared and translated the original documents, including necessary collations. He also wrote the introductory and explanatory material. Kent Harold Richards edited the manuscript on behalf of the series.

BURKE O. LONG

Chronological Table

IMPERIAL POWERS	JUDAH	DATES	TEXTS	EVENTS
ASSYRIA				
Esarhaddon (680–669)				
Ashurbanipal (668–627)	Josiah (640–609)	650	#1	
Sin-shar-ishkun (?–612)			ch. 6	
Ashur-uballit II (611–609)	Jehoahaz (609)			612–609 Fall of Assyria
BABYLONIA				
Nabopolassar (625–605)	Jehoiakim (609–598)		#52?	
Nebuchadrezzar II (604–562)	Jehoiachin (598/597)	600	#2	597 Judah surrenders
	Zedekiah (597–587)		ch. 7	First deportation
			#68	587 Fall of Jerusalem
Amel-Marduk (561–560)				
Neriglissar (559–556)			#69	Babylonian Exile
Labashi-Marduk (556)				
Nabonidus (555–539)		550		

PERSIA	JUDAH (Governors)	EGYPT (Satraps)		PALESTINE AND EGYPT	GREECE AND ASIA MINOR
Cyrus (550–530)	Shesh-bazzar (c. 538)			540 Babylon falls to Cyrus 539 Return of Judean exiles	
Cambyses (529–522)		Aryandes		525 Cambyses conquers Egypt 520–515 Jerusalem Temple rebuilt	
Darius I (521–486)	Zerubbabel (515) Elnathan (late 6th)	Farnadata (–486?)	500 / ch. 2 / #70	486–83 Egypt rebels	499 Rebellion of Ionian cities 490 Persian defeat at Marathon 480 Persia invades Greece, defeated at Salamis
Xerxes I (485–465)	Ahzai (early 5th)	Achaemenes (481?–459)	ch. 3	465–54 Egypt rebels (Inaros)	
Artaxerxes I (464–424)	Ezra ? Nehemiah (445–?)	Arshama (454–403?)	450	Sin-uballit (Sanballat) governor of Samaria	459–456 Herodotus visits Egypt 448 Rebellion of Megabyzus in Asia Minor
Xerxes II (424)	Bagavahya		#11	410–407 Arshama on leave in Persia 410 Elephantine Temple destroyed	431–404 Peloponnesian Wars
Darius II (423–405)			ch. 4 / ch. 5	404 Egypt rebels (Amyrtaeus) 399 Accession of Nepherites	
Artaxerxes II (404–359)			400		

To Sardis

R. Halys

Royal Road

TAURUS MTS

Amida

Carchemish

Haran

Guzanu

Mt. Amanus

Aleppo

R. Balih

BIT ADINI

Ninev

Orontes

R. Habur

Mt. Lebanon

Hamath

Ashur

Mediterranean Sea

ASSYRIA

Byblos

Anti-Lebanon

A B A R   N A H A R A

R. Euphrates

Nakhthor's
Route*

Damascus

Hazor

Megiddo

R. Jordan

B

Dead Sea

SINAI

*Text No. 41

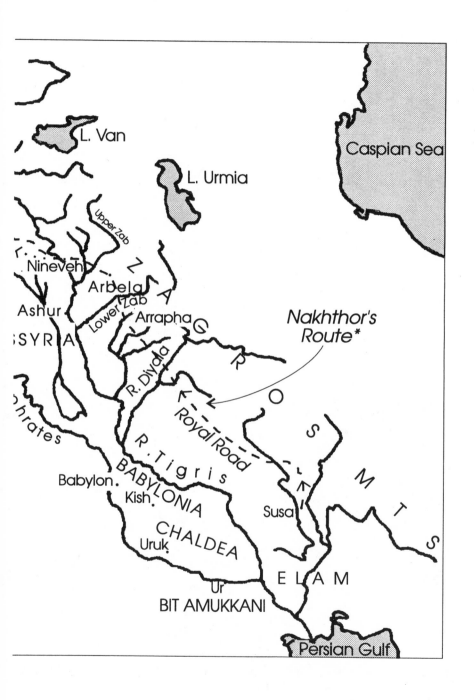

L. Van

L. Urmia

Caspian Sea

Upper Zab

Nineveh

Arbela

Lower Zab

Ashur

Arrapha

SSYRIA

Nakhthor's
Route*

R. Divala

Royal Road

R. Tigris

Babylon.

BABYLONIA

Kish.

CHALDEA

Uruk.

Susa

ELAM

Ur

BIT AMUKKANI

Persian Gulf

Z

A

G

R

O

S

M

T

S

hrates

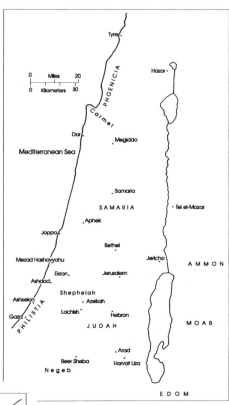

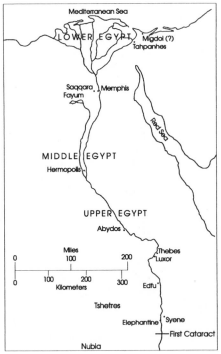

Abbreviations

AAB	*An Aramaic Bibliography*, I (Fitzmyer and Kaufman 1992)
AD	*Aramaic Documents of the Fifth Century B.C.* (Driver 1954, 1965)
AIBL	Académie des Inscriptions et Belles-lettres, Paris
AP	*Aramaic Papyri of the Fifth Century B.C.* (Cowley 1923)
Arch. Mus.	Archaeological Museum, Cairo University
BA	*The Biblical Archaeologist*
BM	British Museum, London
BMAP	*The Brooklyn Museum Aramaic Papyri* (Kraeling 1953)
CIS	*Corpus inscriptionum semiticarum* (AIBL 1889)
Clermont-Ganneau	Clermont-Ganneau Collection, AIBL, Paris
DAE	*Documents araméens d'Égypte* (Grelot 1972)
Eg. Mus.	Egyptian Museum, Cairo
EVV	English versions of the Bible
IEJ	*Israel Exploration Journal*
IM	Israel Museum, Jerusalem
JAOS	*Journal of the American Oriental Society*
JBL	*Journal of Biblical Literature*
JNES	*Journal of Near Eastern Studies*
JUM	Jordan University Museum, Amman
Lib.	Library
O.	Ostracon
P.	Papyrus
RES	*Répertoire d'épigraphie sémitique* (AIBL 1900–1968)
St. Mus.	Staatliche Museen, Berlin

TADA   *Textbook of Aramaic Documents from Ancient Egypt*, I
        (Porten and Yardeni 1986)
VA   Vorderasiatische Abteilung

Scribal Abbreviations in Original Texts

א׳   ארדבן ,ארדב   Ardab(s)
ב׳   בת   Bath(s)
ש׳   שקל, שקלם, תקל, תקלן   Shekel(s)
√   *letek* (one half *homer*)
Ⱶ   *homer*

Explanation of Signs

[. . .]   Gap in the Hebrew and Aramaic text. The approximate length of the gap is indicated in the original texts, not in the translation.

[שלם]   Single brackets enclose restorations.

שׁ   Damaged letter, the identification of which is reasonably certain.

[שׁ]   Visible traces suitable to the restored letter, but not necessarily requiring it.

[֯]   Trace of an unidentifiable letter.

כי . זכר   Dot indicates a word divider in the original.

‹ ›   Modern editorial addition.

{ }   Modern editorial deletion.

{{ }}   Erasure by the ancient scribe.

ˆשלםˆ   Supralinear addition by the ancient scribe.

/   Editorial separation of two words written without an intervening space.

[*At sunset*]   Italics indicate translation of words conjecturally restored, or the assumed sense where no original can be restored. Also used for editorial comment. For example: [*Several names are lost*].

שׁ′, etc.   Abbreviation in the original. See list of abbreviations.

Introduction

I. Overview

This volume contains most of the letters extant in Aramaic and Hebrew (excluding those found in the Hebrew Bible) down to the time of Alexander the Great. In addition there is one letter each in Edomite, Ammonite, and Phoenician, the only extant letters in those languages.

In general intent the book is similar to Edward Wente, *Letters from Ancient Egypt* (WAW 1). There are, however, two significant differences. The first concerns cultural coherence. Egypt was a highly integrated society—complex but coherent throughout its millennia-long history. The phrase "Egyptian culture" means something we can define. The same is true of ancient "Hebrew culture," the milieu of the letters in chapters 6–7. These Hebrew letters, in fact, were written in the space of a single generation, by Jewish correspondents most of whom lived in southern Judah only a few miles from each other. The case of the Aramaic letters—nearly three-quarters of this collection—is quite different. There is no such underlying cultural unity, despite the fact that the Aramaic correspondence covers a much shorter time span than the Egyptian, some 250 years as opposed to nearly fifteen hundred. "Aramean culture" can be defined in terms of inscriptions and archaeological remains, to be sure. However, that tells us almost nothing about the cultural background of the people who wrote the letters in question, because few if any of those people were native Arameans.

Throughout much of the first millennium, Aramaic, a Semitic language kin to Hebrew and written in a similar alphabetic script, was the dominant language of cross-cultural communication in the Near East. Like Akkadian (Assyrian and Babylonian) in the second millennium and Greek in the Hellenistic age, Aramaic became an international *lingua franca*. From Egypt to Turkey, across Syria and Mesopotamia, even as far away as Pakistan, Aramaic was used for governmental, commercial and personal purposes.

The earliest reliable historical references to Arameans date from the time of Tiglath-Pileser I of Assyria (1115–1077 B.C.E.). His annals relate that he

1

fought with Arameans along the Euphrates west of Babylonia and in the Syrian desert. Arameans appear sporadically in Assyrian and Babylonian texts throughout the succeeding two centuries, sometimes as friendly tribes people, sometimes as hostile "people of the steppe."

In the eighth century B.C.E., when Assyria was the dominant imperial power in the Near East, Arameans were widely dispersed among the other population groups of Mesopotamia. By this time Aramaic was beginning to supplant Akkadian as the dominant spoken language in Mesopotamia. Akkadian remained the official language of the empire, but Aramaic was generally used for diplomatic purposes. By the end of the seventh century, the newly established Babylonian empire was ruled by Aramaic-speaking Chaldeans from southern Iraq. Their successors, the Persians (550–331 B.C.E.), used a number of languages for official purposes, but for general diplomatic and administrative communication, especially with the western part of their empire, Aramaic was the language of choice.

As early as 700 B.C.E., a fairly standardized written form of Aramaic had developed, now known as "Official" or "Imperial" Aramaic. Under Persian auspices, Official Aramaic was taught all across the empire to scribes whose mother tongues ranged from Elamite in the east to Egyptian in the southwest. In addition to this learned scribal usage, a number of dialects of spoken Aramaic were in use in different regions of Mesopotamia, Syria, Palestine, and Egypt.

Under such conditions, it is hardly to be expected that the written language would be uniform. In word formation, vocabulary, and syntax, almost every group of Aramaic texts shows differences, some of them quite pronounced, from other groups. There is a distinct Mesopotamian dialect, for instance (letter No. 1). The Persian administrative correspondence (chapter 5 below) is written in a stilted style full of Persian loanwords.

The closest thing to a common thread in these letters is that of Jewish cultural identity, which links the Aramaic letters in chapters 3–4 to the Hebrew ones in chapters 6–7. But even here, the cultural differences are great: on the one hand, preexilic Palestinian Jews (chapters 6–7); on the other, an isolated postexilic Diaspora community (chapters 3–4).

A second difference from Wente's collection of Egyptian letters is that the present volume includes texts in the original languages, transcribed into unvocalized square script. This should not deter readers who lack knowledge of Hebrew or Aramaic. Neither the translations nor the notes presuppose an ability to read the originals. But the originals are there for the large numbers of readers able to use them.

The seventy letters gathered here come from three historical settings: (1) Assyria in the midst of the civil war that broke out around 650 B.C.E., (2) Syria-Palestine just before and during the Babylonian invasions prior to the fall of Judah and Philistia half a century later, and (3) Egypt in the earlier part of the Persian period, ca. 500–400 B.C.E. The Aramaic letters appear first, then the Hebrew, and finally the Canaanite. Within these groupings, the arrangement is roughly chronological.

II. Epistolary Style and Conventions

The style and conventions of ancient Near Eastern letter writing (including the Greek papyri from Hellenistic Egypt) have been extensively studied for nearly a century. It is beyond the scope of this introduction to attempt a thorough form-critical analysis of the Aramaic, Hebrew, and Canaanite letters. The reader interested in pursuing the subject of epistolography in greater detail may consult the studies of Fitzmyer (1981) and Pardee (1982: 153–64) on epistolary structure and formulas, and Porten (1979; 1980) on the physical details of writing on papyrus and leather.

A letter can be broadly defined as a written communication sent by one person or a group of people to another person or group. This implies that the persons are separated by sufficient distance to prevent them from communicating orally. Typically, letters contain greetings, instructions, requests, and information.

The content of the letters in this anthology is immensely varied. There are short, informal notes between family members and friends about such commonplace topics as shopping for salt (No. 24), mixing dough (No. 19), and shearing sheep (No. 15). There are postcard-style letters "just to say hello" (e.g., No. 9). There are more extended letters on family finances and commercial ventures (chapter 2). Some contain vivid personal details. Several people have just been arrested (Nos. 14 and 40) or released from jail (Nos. 7, 31, and 32), one correspondent is recovering from snakebite (No. 7), another pettishly complains that he does not like the tunic his mother has sent him (No. 5)!

In earlier periods of Egyptian history, the rate of literacy among women was considerably lower than it was among men. Some of the Egyptian letters intended for women have an external address in a man's name, suggesting that the recipients needed to have the letters read to them by a man in the household (Wente 1990: 8–9). In the fifth-century Aramaic family correspondence from Egypt (chapters 2 and 3), several letters are written to women, with no suggestion that the recipients were unable to read them for themselves.

Many of the letters deal with military matters: requests for reinforcements, reports on troop movements and missions carried out, intelligence information, requisitions for rations and men, concerns about morale. Virtually all of the letters in chapters 1 and 7 are written by soldiers, or concern military affairs. A few touch on religious matters such as the observance of Sabbath (No. 22), the celebration of Passover and Unleavened Bread (Nos. 19 and 30), and the events surrounding the destruction of the Jewish temple at Elephantine (Nos. 33–36). There are also bureaucratic letters between Persian officials, written in a "rubber-stamp" style in which an earlier letter is quoted and action is briefly authorized (chapter 5).

III. Letter Writing Materials

Classified according to the materials on which they are written, the letters fall into three groups. First, there are ostraca, letters inked on broken pieces of clay pottery (No. 1; chapters 3, 6–7; Nos. 78–79). The term is sometimes used broadly to include texts written on limestone flakes, but none of the Aramaic letters are written on this material. Typically, Hebrew and Aramaic ostraca are small, ranging from about half the size of the palm of one's hand to the size of two palms held together, and containing from four to a dozen or more short lines of writing. Sometimes only one side (normally the concave) is inscribed, though many letters continue on the convex side. Occasionally the convex and concave contain two entirely different letters.

No. 1 is an ostracon of unique size, far out of proportion with anything else in the collection. Written on a thick piece of a heavy storage jar, it originally measured about 43 by 60 centimeters (17 inches high by almost 2 feet wide), and contained over twenty long lines, though much of it is now lost. The enormous size of this ostracon is perhaps to be explained from the unusual circumstances of the writer. The other ostraca were all written in towns. In an urban setting, small potsherds could always be found lying about in the streets, and such ostraca were invariably used for writing short notes. For longer correspondence, papyrus or leather was the normal medium. Where the author of letter No. 1 was when he wrote is unknown, but he had just returned from assignment in the desolate marshes of southern Babylonia and needed to make a lengthy and important report. He may simply have had no access to a friendly urban center where he could buy leather or papyrus, or find a scribe competent to write the letter in cuneiform on a clay tablet.

Leather is the second material used for letters. Although only a dozen letters in this collection are written on leather (chapter 5), this material was widely used in Mesopotamia for writing Aramaic. A common motif in Assyrian military art is a pair of scribes standing side by side recording the results of a campaign. One scribe, who is typically bearded, holds a clay tablet on which he is writing in cuneiform with a stylus. The other, clean-shaven, writes with a pen on soft material. The second scribe can only be writing in Aramaic, and the soft material is most probably leather. Akkadian texts of the period refer to "scribes who write on skins" (Driver 1965: 1).

No Aramaic documents on leather have survived in Mesopotamia, but the letters in chapter 5 were written either there or in Persia. The leather is stretched thin and appears to have been carefully prepared for writing. It is sometimes described as "parchment," though whether the term is appropriate is largely a matter of definition. It is hardly comparable in quality to good medieval parchment, though no doubt it was the best available at the time.

The third writing material, papyrus, was extensively used in Egypt from very ancient times. Papyrus was made from specially prepared reeds sliced lengthwise, laid out in a grid of vertical strips covered by horizontal strips, then pressed and polished into sheets. These were glued together twenty at a time to form a roll. Papyrus was the most convenient and relatively inexpensive soft writing material known in antiquity. Aside from the ostraca, all of the Aramaic letters written in Egypt (and No. 2 from Philistia) are written on it. Papyrus may also have been used to a limited extent in Mesopotamia, but no Aramaic papyri have been found there. It could not be made locally, and the difficulty of importing it from Egypt would have kept it from being common.

IV. Writing a Letter

A scribe writing a letter on papyrus followed a standard procedure. He would first take a papyrus roll, ordinarily from 25 to 32 centimeters (about 10 to 13 inches) wide. Holding the roll in a horizontal position, the scribe would roll off a length and cut it into a new sheet of the desired height. The letter would be begun on the *recto,* the side originally inside the roll, where the papyrus fibers run perpendicular to the joins. When the recto was filled, the papyrus would be flipped over top to bottom, and the text continued on the *verso* (upside down relative to the recto). A large space would be left at the bottom of the verso for the external address.

When the letter was completed, it would be turned recto-up and folded upward toward the top in a series of horizontal bands, so that the blank space left at the bottom of the verso could be flapped over and exposed. The address would be written on this space. The letter, now folded into one long narrow strip, would then be folded laterally into quarters or halves (in a few cases, thirds), bound with string, and sealed with a lump of wet clay impressed with the seal of the writer. It was now ready for dispatch.

The process was similar with letters on leather, except that the text would be written entirely on the smooth side of the skin. The hair side, corresponding to the verso of a papyrus, was more difficult to write on because of its rougher texture and would not be inscribed, except for the external address and a docket (see below). For an interesting and very detailed account of the manner of writing and folding letters, and how this knowledge is used in reconstructing damaged documents, see Porten (1979; 1980; with numerous illustrations by Ada Yardeni).

V. The Form of a Letter

In broad outline, the letter has three main parts: an opening, which may include an address and a greeting; a body; and a closing, with certain concluding formulas and additional information. The form of a typical letter may be diagrammed as follows:

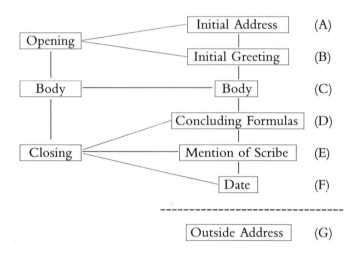

Any of these elements may be omitted. Some letters (e.g., No. 9) consist entirely of greeting formulas with no other message. Other short notes contain only the body, a bare message with no opening or closing formalities (e.g., Nos. 12, 23). Let us now examine each of these elements in a little more detail.

A. Initial Address

The first part of the letter is the "initial address," often referred to by the Latin term *praescriptio.* Except for very informal notes, this element is nearly always found in the Aramaic letters. A number of the Hebrew letters from Lachish lack it. The initial address identifies the sender and the recipient. It can be formulated in different ways, with either name coming first, but the most common form is "to A from B." Titles of sender and addressee may be included, especially in more formal correspondence. Such words as "lord," "servant," and terms of family relationship are frequent. In the Hebrew letters there is no formal line between the initial address and the greeting. Instead, there are several formulas incorporating both elements (see below).

The three Canaanite letters all begin with a "double-saying" formula. A literal translation of the opening words of No. 68 (Edomite) would be approximately

"A saying (?) of Lumalak; say to Bulbul . . . ." The beginnings of Nos. 69 and
70 are similar, though the phraseology differs slightly in each case. The lack
of written vowels makes it impossible to distinguish between the noun "a saying
(of)," the indicative verb "he says" (the same consonants may also be read "she
says" in Phoenician), and the imperative "say!" However the words are parsed,
the double use of the root word for speech is unlike anything found in Aramaic
and Hebrew correspondence. Whether this distinctive formulation goes back
to an old Canaanite model, or whether it derives from Akkadian, we do not
know. Ugaritic letters from the thirteenth century B.C.E. also use a "double-
saying" formula, though it is not identical.

The addresses of the Aramaic letters sometimes use familial language in an
honorific sense that does not correspond to the actual relationship of the
correspondents; see the similar use of "your brother" and "your son" in two
Hebrew letters from Arad (Nos. 51, 60). Occasionally, as in several of the
Elephantine ostraca, the initial address is omitted. In these cases, we may assume
that the letter-carrier was given verbal instructions concerning delivery.
Characteristically, the word "greetings!" (literally, "peace") follows the names
in many of the Aramaic texts.

There is an additional opening feature in most of the letters in chapter 2,
also found occasionally in late Babylonian letters. At the very beginning, before
the initial address, there is a "temple greeting," a word directed to a local shrine
in the addressee's town, as for example, "Greetings to the temple of Nabu"
(No. 3), "Greetings to the temple of Banit at Syene" (No. 6), "Greetings to
the temple of YHW at Elephantine" (No. 10).

B. Initial Greeting

This is a word of greeting, well-wishing, or both. In its simplest form it
may consist simply of the word "greetings," as noted above. Sometimes the
greetings become elaborate formulas, as in No. 34, "May the God of Heaven
bless our lord always, and may he put you in the good graces of King Darius
and his household a thousand times more than now. May he grant you long
life, and may you always be happy and strong." Between these two extremes
a variety of forms occur.

There are two major types of Aramaic greeting formulas. One uses the verb
"bless" (e.g., "We bless you by Ptah—may he let us see you again in good health,"
No. 8); the other uses various phrases with the word "peace," sometimes
translated "well-being" or "greetings" depending on context (e.g., "I send you
greetings and best wishes for your good health," No. 37). Both types of
formulas are sometimes found side by side in the same letter.

Many of the Hebrew letters have no greeting formulas. Those that occur
are unlike those found in Aramaic. The preferred formula at Lachish uses the
verb "hear": "May YHWH send you (literally, 'cause you to hear') good news
this very day" (No. 61; cf. Nos. 62–63, 66–67). A variant formula appears in

No. 64, where the Hebrew original of the phrase "May YHWH make this time a good one for you," actually uses a form of the verb "see." In Nos. 61, 64, and 66, the greeting formula is directly followed by a formula of self-abasement: "I am nothing but a dog." In the Arad letters, a different opening phrase combines the address with a "greeting-plus-blessing" formula: "A sends greetings to (literally, 'sends to greet') B" followed by "I bless you by YHWH!" (Nos. 51, 54, 60). This is once replaced by a simple "To A—May YHWH bless you," (literally, "ask for your peace," No. 55). In the Canaanite letters, the greeting seems to take the form of a question, "Are you well?" to which the writer of No. 70 adds, "I am."

C. Body

The bodies of the letters are as varied in length and content as are people's motives in writing to each other. One fairly common element is a "secondary greeting," a greeting to be relayed to someone other than the addressee, for example: "Greetings to Shabbetai son of Shug. Greetings to Pasai . . . Greetings to the whole neighborhood" (No. 5). Secondary greetings may appear anywhere in the body of the letter, but characteristically they are found at the beginning.

D.–F. Concluding Formulas

Many Aramaic letters have no formal conclusion, and none of the Hebrew or Canaanite ones do. They simply stop when the message is concluded. Some of the Aramaic letters add the concluding sentence "I am sending this letter to greet you" (or ". . . for your peace of mind," Nos. 3–9, 11, 20). The administrative letters in chapter 5 typically record the name of the scribe who wrote the copy (E on the diagram above) and sometimes other persons such as the official who drafted it (No. 40) or persons receiving copies for reference ("so-and-so has been informed . . . ," Nos. 38, 41–44). A date (F on the diagram) is not a regular part of Aramaic and Hebrew letters, but some very formal correspondence is dated (e.g., "20th of Marheshwan, 17th year of King Darius," No. 34; cf. No. 49). When a date is given, it usually appears near the end, though in one case it is found after the initial greeting (No. 30).

G. Outside Address

A letter on soft material required an address that could be read from the outside without breaking the seal. Usually the names of both sender and addressee appear, sometimes with slightly different wording and titles from those used inside. Administrative letters (chapter 5) generally add a docket, a brief indication of contents. The Hermopolis papyri (chapter 2) have an additional phrase specifying the location of the addressee, for example, "Let it be carried to Syene."

Despite the lack of cultural homogeneity, there is sufficient commonality in the structure and formulation of these letters to justify our speaking broadly of a common epistolary tradition. In particular, there are similar ways of formulating addresses and greetings which cut across lines of language and historical setting.

VI. Text and Translation Style

The textual bases of this collection are as follows: for the Aramaic papyri (and the documents on leather), the text is based on Porten and Yardeni 1986. This edition has been collated with published photographs and, when possible, examination of the original texts. Notes indicate where my reading differs significantly from that of Porten and Yardeni. The Hebrew letters and the Phoenician letter are based on the edition of Pardee 1982, with the same qualifications. The readings of the Aramaic ostraca are my own. Originals were examined and new photographs taken whenever possible. For the Ammonite and Edomite letters, only preliminary publications are available.

The originals of these letters can be read and understood reasonably well, but there are limiting factors. Each letter is unique; only one copy exists. (The only exception is No. 34, of which there are two copies.) Thus, when a manuscript is damaged, as many are, there is no parallel textual tradition to which one may turn for help in restoring the gaps.

The most fragmentary letters are barely intelligible and nearly all have been excluded. A few badly damaged letters are included in the collection because of their great intrinsic interest. No. 31, the so-called Passover papyrus, is a significant historical document because of the light it sheds on Jewish ritual observance in the postexilic Diaspora, despite its being so broken and faded that even the word "Passover" has to be restored. The case is similar with the Ashur ostracon (No. 1), the only Aramaic letter from ancient Assyria, and the Adon papyrus (No. 2), which parallels biblical evidence for the Babylonian advance into Syria-Palestine just before Judah and Philistia fell to Nebuchadrez-zar. A tiny Hebrew fragment of an ostracon from Arad (No. 52) appears to be a remnant of an accession proclamation of one of the kings of Judah (probably Jehoahaz or Jehoiakim), and an equally fragmentary piece from Lachish (No. 65), bears a tantalizing reference to a certain "[. . . ya]hu the prophet," a contemporary of Jeremiah.

The accuracy with which missing words can be restored to damaged texts varies a good deal from case to case. Sometimes common epistolary phrases and honorific titles can be restored with confidence. On other occasions, a knowledge of the writers' historical circumstances and the social conventions of the period permits plausible conjectures to be made as to the general content of missing phrases. But in some cases one is reduced to guesswork, try-ing to make sense of the parts that remain on the basis of an intuitive sense of what *might* have been in the lost passages. Restorations of Aramaic or Hebrew readings are indicated by enclosing the translation in square brackets. A purely conjectural restoration is further indicated by printing the English in italics.

A second limiting factor is vocabulary. For the Hebrew letters, that is only occasionally a problem, but even the earliest Aramaic inscriptions show a mixed vocabulary. Imperial Aramaic was used over many generations in different regions and for different purposes by many persons for whom Aramaic was a second language. There are marked dialectal differences among different groups of these letters, and we find in them loanwords from a number of different Near Eastern languages.

The Ashur ostracon (No. 1) contains borrowings from Akkadian not found anywhere else in Aramaic. The letters from the Persian chancery (chapter 5) use numerous Persian words, especially administrative titles, but some every-day words as well. The texts from Egypt contain Egyptian loanwords; one letter (No. 49) is so riddled with Egyptian boatyard jargon that we can barely understand it.

Sometimes the meanings of these foreign loanwords are known; sometimes not. Where they are, they are generally translated without comment. Where the sense is uncertain or debated, an explanatory note is added. Where the meaning is unknown, it is indicated by ellipsis or a rough approximation in italics, but the use of brackets, italics, ellipses, and notes has been kept to a bare minimum.

Although the literary level of these letters is not high, they are by no means devoid of color. There are moments of sustained narrative power (the eye-witness narrative of the destruction of the Jewish temple at Elephantine [No. 34]), flashes of wit (Bel-etir's laconic account of his audience with Ashur-banipal, in which the king wryly quotes him a proverb [No. 1]), passages of rhetorical vehemence (Adon's impassioned plea for military aid [No. 2], or the awkward eloquence of a Judean field hand's petition to recover a confiscated garment [No. 50]). There is even some sustained sarcasm, as a subordinate officer at Lachish repeatedly addresses his commander in the most insubordinate manner (No. 64 and especially No. 62).

In keeping with the intent of this series, word order and sentence structure in the translations strive for idiomatic English, even when the Aramaic and Hebrew originals are formulated rather differently. The short, choppy clauses and sentences that characterize some of the originals are often linked to form longer English sentences. Occasionally, long rambling sentences in the original are broken into two or more shorter English sentences.

It is characteristic of ancient Semitic style not to spell out the logical and syntactical links that are normally made explicit in European languages. Sometimes these nuances are expressed in the originals by variations in word order; sometimes they are merely implicit. Aramaic and Hebrew frequently form long chains of sentences by repeating a single all-purpose conjunction over and over again. To avoid a monotonous and un-English series of "ands," the ubiquitous conjunction is often omitted in translation. Elsewhere its presence is indicated by any of several English words or by various subordinating and coordinating constructions.

Aramaic and Hebrew writers often use the expression "now" or "and now" to begin a new section of a letter or to introduce a new topic, where in English this is indicated by beginning a new paragraph, or in some cases by starting a new sentence within the same paragraph. Some of the Aramaic letters use demonstrative pronouns much more frequently than is normal in English: for example, "these soldiers," where we would say "the soldiers"; "that Vidranga," where English style prefers simply "Vidranga." In these cases, common English usage has been followed.

The words "your servant" and "my lord" present a special problem. These words belong to the stylized conventions of ancient Near Easter letter writing and sometimes appear repeatedly throughout a letter. Often the translations reproduce the clichés only where they first occur, thereafter substituting "I" and "you." In a few cases, however, the formulas are repeated in English each time they appear.

The choice was made in each instance on the basis of the translator's sense of the tone of the letter. Where it is a simple matter of the normal conventions of address by an inferior to a superior, using the formula once in the translation suffices. Obsequious tone, as in No. 50, is reflected by repeating the English phrases each time they occur in the original. Where the writer is being ironic or sarcastic, as in No. 62, one is even tempted to place the words "your servant" in quotation marks. The reader may contrast the rendering of the "servant-lord" formulas in the Adon letter (No. 2) and the Yavneh-Yam petition (No. 50) on the one hand, and the Lachish letters (chap. 7) on the other. In general, an attempt has been made to match the style of each translation — whether stilted, formal, less formal, casual, or downright colloquial — to the style of the original.

In a few cases, footnotes give a literal rendering of expressions translated more idiomatically in the body of the text. The student may find them useful, and the general reader may be interested to see how these turns of phrase are expressed in the original.

* * *

Generous financial assistance for research expenses has been provided by the National Endowment for the Humanities and the H. R. MacMillan Foundation (Vancouver). I must express a particular debt of gratitude to Kent H. Richards for his skilled editorial oversight at all stages of preparation of the manuscript. Thanks are due to the series editor, Burke O. Long, for his encouragement and his valuable suggestions on the style and scope of the introductory material, as well as his patience in waiting for a manuscript that was long coming. I am also indebted to my former teacher Delbert R. Hillers, whose careful critique of the readings and translations led to their improvement at many points. No doubt this would be a much better book if I had taken their advice more often.

This book is dedicated to my parents, John Blackwell Lindenberger and Virginia Gray Lindenberger.

Translations

I

Aramaic Diplomatic-Military Correspondence

═══════════ Introduction ═══════════

The first two letters have little in common beyond the fact that both come from the seventh century and that both may be broadly defined as diplomatic and military correspondence. No. 1 comes from mid-seventh-century Assyria. No. 2, from the end of that century, was written from Palestine to Egypt. The correspondents are persons of different status: army officers in the former case, kings in the latter. Even the materials on which the two letters are written are different: potsherd and papyrus, respectively.

Letter No. 1 is unique. The number of letters surviving from this period in Assyrian history runs into the thousands, and they are written in Akkadian or neo-Assyrian. This letter is the only one yet found in Aramaic. It was written with pen and ink on a very large ostracon, a piece of a broken storage jar. Discovered at the site of ancient Ashur during the German excavations of 1903–1913, the text is in a poor state of preservation. It was found broken into six fragments with some portions missing. An entire piece of the left margin is completely lost. The effects of groundwater and chemicals have left parts of the remaining surface illegible. Comparison of the original now with photographs taken half a century ago shows that the ink has faded considerably in the interim.

To reconstruct a text that is even partly coherent requires more extensive conjecture than is the rule elsewhere in this volume. Insofar as possible, restorations are based on known phraseology from neo-Assyrian documents and other Aramaic letters, taking account of the physical length of the lacunae. But those neo-Assyrian texts are in a different language, and the other Aramaic letters (with the exception of No. 2)

15

are from well over a century later. Thus, the level of uncertainty in the translation of Letter No. 1 is high.

This letter was written on the eve of the outbreak of a major civil conflict in Mesopotamia. During the reign of King Esarhaddon of Assyria (680–669 B.C.E.), Assyrian hegemony over Babylonia was firmly established. Babylonia had once been a great independent nation, and there was still a strong undercurrent of separatist sentiment.

To head off the prospect of Babylonian secession at his death, Esarhaddon contrived an unusual plan. Against the advice of some of his counselors, he designated two sons as crown princes: Ashurbanipal was to succeed him on the Assyrian throne in Nineveh, but Shamash-shum-ukin was to be "king" in Babylon. We do not know which brother was the elder; there is some evidence that they may have been twins (Wiseman 1958: 7; Kaufman 1974: 106). In real terms, the arrangement meant that Ashurbanipal was imperial ruler of Assyria. Shamash-shum-ukin, though not technically his brother's vassal, was the junior partner, little more than a military governor. Thus the fiction of a "king" in Babylonia was maintained.

Esarhaddon's vassals were required to swear loyalty oaths to him, calling down curses upon themselves if they should ever rebel. Shamash-shum-ukin did not himself have to swear fealty, but was present at the ceremony.

For nearly eighteen years after Esarhaddon's death, the arrangement worked. Yet Babylonian nationalism was on the rise in the southern cities. At the same time, dissident Aramean (Chaldean) tribes in southern Babylonia were becoming more and more restive. Foremost among them was Bit-Amukkani, a tribe that lived in the marshy hinterland south of the city of Babylon. The Aramean marsh- and desert-dwellers and the urban Babylonian nationalists had little in common culturally, but were able to join forces on one key point: opposition to Assyrian rule.

In 651, open war broke out between Assyria and Babylonia, with Shamash-shum-ukin leading the combined rebel forces in the south. Hostilities lasted until 648, when the Assyrians regained the upper hand. In that year, Shamash-shum-ukin and the remnants of his army were blockaded in Babylon and reduced to starvation. In the closing days of the siege, the palace was set afire, and Shamash-shum-ukin perished in the blaze, possibly by his own hand. (The complex course of the war has been studied exhaustively by Dietrich [1970]; for a shorter summary, see Saggs 1968: 138–41.)

Letter No. 1 appears to date from just before the outbreak of war in 651. The situation in Babylonia is already unstable. Shamash-shum-ukin has not yet broken openly with Assyria but has opened secret negotiations with the tribal leaders of Bit-Amukkani, seeking their support.

The reconstructed letter is a report from an Assyrian officer named Bel-etir to a fellow officer, Pir-Amurri, who is evidently in the Assyrian city of Ashur. Both men are loyal to Ashurbanipal and have served together in the past. Bel-etir has been on special assignment in southern Babylonia tracking small groups of rebel Assyrian soldiers who are serving as couriers in the clandestine negotiations between Shamash-shum-ukin and Bit-Amukkani.

Bel-etir reports a substantial intelligence coup: he has captured four messengers in the remote desert and discovered that they were carrying a letter implicating Shamash-shum-ukin in the incipient uprising. What follows is only partly intelligible, but there seems to be a reference to a fifth conspirator who was captured separately. The prisoners were taken by Bel-etir to Ashurbanipal at an unknown location somewhere in the south. The captives' ordeal is described in detail. They were publicly humiliated by being tied up with the dogs in the town square (cf. the curse pronounced on Vidranga in No. 34). They were then branded, interrogated, and turned over to Bel-etir as slaves. Bel-etir summarizes the evidence against them: they were caught in rebel territory (*prima facie* confirmation of their guilt); the brands on their arms were there to see; and they confessed to having gone over to the anti-Assyrian opposition. An additional piece of evidence mentioned is a letter from the first four prisoners to a certain Abbaya, a rebel leader in the far south. Whether this is the confiscated letter already mentioned or a second one is unclear.

The rebels, possibly destined for eventual execution, seem to have been given a reprieve through a surprise action by another officer. A certain Upaqa-ana-arbail, without Bel-etir's knowledge and for unstated reasons, has had some of the men transported north to Ashur. Perhaps he was simply an overzealous subordinate who wished to have them interrogated at army headquarters. Bel-etir orders curtly that they be sent back at once. Expecting opposition from someone named Apil-esharra, perhaps Upaqa-ana-arbail's superior at Ashur, Bel-etir observes that the prisoners themselves can be made to confirm his story.

A fourth officer, Naid-Marduk, is being sent by Bel-etir to Ashur to overtake the prisoner convoy and bring them back. Several additional names are mentioned of persons who are to be returned to Babylonia. Again the reasons are not given. They may be rebels from Assyria's northern possessions, being sent south into exile or for public execution.

There follows a stylized list of four successive Assyrian rulers who exiled persons from various places, followed by a badly broken passage referring to the punishment of traitors. The meaning of the words translated "burn" and "burning" is uncertain, but they may allude to a widely attested ancient Near Eastern curse directed against a rebellious vassal: death by fire. If so, this part of the letter, with its solemn style, list of royal precedents, and reference to treaty curses, is a virtual death sentence for the prisoners in question. Little is clear in the final lines, except that someone is angry at the writer and that something is said about a place called Bit-Dibla.

Half a century separates this letter from No. 2. During the interim, major upheavals occurred in Near Eastern politics. By the end of the seventh century, Assyria had collapsed and Babylonia was now the ascendant power. The neo-Babylonian empire was flourishing under the recently instituted kingship of the Chaldeans, descendants of the same south Babylonian tribes who had supported Shamash-shum-ukin's abortive war of independence.

The new military leader was Nebuchadrezzar (Nebuchadnezzar). In 605 while still crown prince, Nebuchadrezzar defeated the Egyptian armies at Carchemish and Hamath in Syria. By 604, now sole ruler in Babylonia after the death of his father Nabopolassar, he was again on the march, aiming to extend Babylonian influence down the Syro-Palestinian coast to the Egyptian border. The events of these years are well documented, both in the Babylonian Chronicle (Wiseman 1956) and the Hebrew Bible (especially 2 Kgs 24:1–7 and Jeremiah 46–47).

Letter No. 2 was written in the midst of this chaotic situation by one Adon, ruler of one of the coastal city-states lying in Nebuchadrezzar's path, probably Ekron (Porten

1981). In great consternation he appeals to his overlord, the Egyptian pharaoh Necho II (610–594), for military aid, reminding the Egyptian that he, Adon, has been a faithful vassal and as such is entitled to support.

The letter reached its destination. The papyrus, found at Saqqara, bears a notation in Demotic jotted by an Egyptian file clerk. The appeal, however, was to no avail. Necho was in no position to help his desperate vassal. There were no auxiliary troops to send, and within short order all of the coastal cities were forced to capitulate to the Babylonian army.

══════ Report of an Assyrian Officer ══════

1. Ashur Ostracon (Berlin St. Mus. VA 8384)*
(Ashur, c. 650 B.C.E.)

1   ‏[אל א]חי פרור אחוך בלטר שלם לש[נ]לחת עלי מן זין]

2   ‏[הוית] עמי את במתכדי ואנה וערבי ומֹן . . . אתן בית]

3   ‏[אוכן אזי אזל]ת מן ארך עם גרצפן ועם וגמֹר אןֹ . . . . . .]

4   ‏אנה [רדף קרקן ב]בית אוכן 4 המו אגרת מלך בכל [הות]

5   ‏ביד{הֹ}[ֹיֹה]ם י[העבדן מרד ב]בית אוכן בחפירֹו במדברא אחזן
המ[ו . . . . .]

6   ‏איתֹ[ית] / המ[ו . . . . . ואגרתא ה]וֹשרת למרֹי מלכאֹ אזי [נברן] אחזן מן
נֹה[ן . . . . .]

7   ‏ואתית [עם כלהם] קֹדם [מראֹ]י מל[כא בארחן] עם כלביא שמן יהֹב המו
לי מראֹיֹ מלכאֹן עבדן]

8   ‏כי / זא {זא} אמר לי מראי מלכא לאֹמר [זלך] המו ולטחנו לה
ֹיֹטעם / כאֹ חֹזית בנֹעינין זילי מן]

9   ‏בית אֹוֹכן המו ידיהם כתבת וקימת קדמי קן[יֹמֹ] קרקן הלו בבית אוכן /
המו מן יד{הֹ}ֹיֹ[ה]ם אחדת אגרת]

10   ‏אבֹי יאמֹרֹ לאמר מן שמהיקר [נ]בוֹזרכן אחשן[ין] וולול נבוזרכן
ואחשי אפקנרביל שם [במסנר ב . . . . .]

11   ‏וולֹוֹל שמהיקר ואבי הלו הֹ[נושר] כזי יאתה אפקנרביל אשור מן עקב
יהתב המו לאפק[ן . . . . . . ← ?] והן]

* The sign [? ← . . .] indicates a lacuna of uncertain length at the left edge of a column.

12 פלסר [ויש]אל הצדא הני מליא אלה בן[לטר] שמי כתב על ידהיהם וקרא
    המו שאל / המו הצד[א . . . . . →?]

13 [. . .]א אל[ה הל]ון עבדן / המו / זלי קרקו הל[ו . .] עם[ן] זי /
    בית / אוכן / המו הלו נדמרדך עזרך שלחת / קד[מ]יהם . . . . . →?]

14 [תהתב] המו אחזא המו הושר / לן אזי בר / נמ[ל] . . .]בֹן ובר
    בן . . .]זֹבן זבנארן ונבושלם זי בית עדן אזי [. . →?]

15 [. . . . . .]ע שבי שבה תכלתפלסר מן בית / אוכן [ושבין] שבה אללי מֹן
    בית עדן ושבי שבה שרכן מן דרסן

16 ושבני שבה סנ[חרב מן כש]ד [. . מלכין] אשֹור יגזֹל[ן . . . . .] מן שֹנֹה
    יקרקן ויכסֹאן / המו וכימן מלכי או[שור . . . . .]

17 בֹן .]דֹיבֹן . . . יאמרן] לאמר קרקי אל תחזו מן[. .]כ.] . . . .] אשֹור
    אשה אכלתהם ומראי מלכא פקרן[. . . . .]

18 למן .]נֹדא אן[. . . .] קרקי אשור יכסֹאן

19 לנבוזרשבֹש ו[. .]ארה מלאכתי אשֹלֹח לך וֹנ[. . . . .]
    הלכתי מלא את לֹבֹת אלהא זי [.]טי[ן . . . . . .]

20 למה לבתי מלא [. . .] וכעת[ן . . . . .] אפיא בֹן . .]קֹן[. . . . .]א[פיא
    כזי תחזה ו[אֹ]א[. .] שנה שלחנֹה [. . . . . .]

21 בבית / דבלא ל[. . .]ו ש[ורד]ן הן . . זי המרתכן[.] זי
    אתן[. . . . .] שורדן זֹי בֹית דֹבֹלֹא

To my brother Pir-amurri from your brother Bel-etir:
Greetings [. . .].

[You have not written to me since] you were with me in Babylonia. I and
Arbayya and [. . . went to Bit-Amukkani. Then] you [left] Uruk with
Ger-sapun and . . .[1] [. . .].

I [was chasing defectors[2] in] Bit-Amukkani. There were four of them. They
had in their possession a letter from the king of Babylon (Shamash-shum-
ukin), and were trying to stir up a rebellion in Bit-Amukkani. We captured
them at Hapiru in the desert. [Then] I brought them [to . . .], and sent [the
letter] to my lord the king (Ashurbanipal). Then we captured [a man from . . .],
and I took [them all][3] before my lord the king [in fetters].

They were put with the dogs.[4] My lord the king gave them to me [as slaves].
For this is what my lord the king said to me, "They are [yours]! As the saying
goes, 'They have ground it, now let them eat it!'"[5]

This is what I have seen [with my own eyes]: They [are from] Bit-Amukkani.
Their arms are inscribed, and they swore an oath in my presence that they

had indeed defected. They were, after all, in Bit-Amukkani! [I also confiscated] from them [a letter to] Abbaya which said, "From Shemeh-yeqar, Nabu-zer-ukin, and Ahishay and Walwal(?)."

Upaqa-ana-arbail has put Nabu-zer-ukin and Ahishay [in prison in . . .], but now I find that he [has had] Walwal(?), Shemeh-yeqar and Abbaya [taken away]. When Upaqa-ana-arbail arrives in Ashur, he is to return them immediately to Apqu [. . .]. If Apil-esharra asks, "Is this report true?" my name "Bel-etir" is inscribed on their arms. Call them in and ask them whether it is true: [. . .] Are they my slaves? Did they defect? Were they with the men from Bit-Amukkani?

I have sent your adjutant Naid-Marduk on ahead of them[6] [. . .]. Send them back; I must deal with them! In addition, send us Bar-[. . .][7] and Bar-[. . .]-zabina, Zaban-iddina and Nabu-ushallim of Bit-Adini. Then [. . .].

Tiglath-pileser	exiled prisoners	from Bit-Amukkani,
Ululai (Shalmaneser V)	exiled [prisoners]	from Bit-Adini,
Sargon	exiled prisoners	from Dur-Sin,
Sennacherib	exiled prisoners	from Chaldea(?),[8]

[. . . the kings of] Assyria would [seize them . . .]. Whenever(?) anyone defected, they would seize them, and burn(?) them. The kings of Assyria would always [. . . and] would say, "Let there be no defectors from me; may a fire devour them! My lord the king has given orders [*that they are indeed to be put to death* . . .] fugitives from Assyria are to be burned(?).

As for Nabu-zer-ushabshi and [. . .]: I will be sending you my report, and [. . .]. Are you really in such a god-awful rage at me that [. . .]? Why are you so angry at me?

Now [. . .]

When you see [. . .], we sent [. . .] at Bit-Dibla [. . .]-shum-iddina of Bit-Dibla.

=========== **Appeal to Pharaoh for Military Aid** ===========

2. Adon Papyrus (Cairo, Eg. Mus. J. 86984 = 3483)
(Saqqara, c. 604 B.C.E.)

A

1 אל מרא מלכן פרעה עבדך אדן מלך עֻ]קרן שלם מרא מלכן פרעה אלהי[ן

2 שמיא וארקא ובעל שמין אלהﬡ רבא ישאלו שנא בכל עדן ויהארכו
יומי[ן

3 פרעה כיומי שמין רֻמין זֻן . . . זֻ[ן] . . . . חילא[ן

4 זי מלך בכל אתו מטאוֹ אפק וֹעﬦ . . . . [

5 [. . . .] אחזו ו֯יׁבלו [. . . . .] בכלן [. . . . .] [. . . . .]

6 כי מרא מלכן פרעה ידע כי עבדך] [. . . . .]

7 למשלח חיל להצלתנׁי֯ אל ישבקנן֯י כי לא שקר עבדך בעדי מרא מלכן]

8 וטבחתה עבדך נצר ונגדא זנה [. . . . .]

9 פחה במתא וספר שנדור סנן] [. . . . .]

B

⟨Demotic⟩ 10

To Pharaoh, Lord of Kings, from your servant King Adon of [Ekron.

May the gods of] heaven and earth and Beel-shemayn [the great] god [seek abundantly at all times the welfare of my lord Pharaoh, Lord of Kings. May they grant] Pharaoh [days as long] as the days of the high heavens!⁹

[. . . The army] of the king of Babylonia has come. They have advanced as far as Aphek, and [. . .]. They have captured [. . .] and have brought [. . .], in all [. . .].

[. . .] for Pharaoh, the Lord of Kings knows that your servant [. . .] to send troops to rescue me. Do not abandon [me, for your servant has not violated the treaty of the Lord of Kings:] your servant has been faithful to his treaty obligations.

Now this commander [. . .] a governor in the land. As for the letter of Sin-duri(?), [. . .].

Demotic Notation: What the ruler of Ekron(?)¹⁰ gave to [. . .].

Notes

1. The name written consonantally as "WGMR" is not known.
2. Literally, "fugitives, runaways," this word refers to persons stirring up rebellion against Assyrian hegemony in Babylonia.
3. Literally, "I went with them before the lord my king in fetters." Since that could not apply to Bel-etir himself, the verb should perhaps be emended to a causative form.
4. Or perhaps "auxiliary troops" (Fales 1987: 468–69).
5. "As the saying goes" is implied. The words that follow appear to be a popular proverb equivalent to "They've made their bed; now let them lie on it!"
6. Or "to you."
7. Evidently a personal name beginning with the Aramaic word "son of." Lemaire

and Durand (1984: 52) discuss this as a distinctive form of dynastic name found among the Aramaic peoples of Syria.

8. Or "Kush."

9. Or (with a different reading of the first letter of the last word) ". . . as the days of the heavens and the waters" (Porten and Yardeni 1986: 6).

10. Ekron is plausible, both graphically and historically (Porten 1981: 43–45).

II

Business and Family Letters

Introduction

The papyrus letters in this chapter make up two small collections of family correspondence that deal with a mixture of personal and business matters. The first group is known as the Hermopolis papyri, after the site where they were discovered in 1945, the ancient Hermopolis Magna (modern Tuna el-Gebel), on the west bank of the Nile about 240 km. (150 mi.) south of Memphis. Six of the seven letters in this group (Nos. 3–8) were dispatched by three men residing in Memphis, all belonging to the same family. The addressees are relatives in the south, in Syene (modern Aswan) and Luxor. No. 9, from a different sender, is also addressed to Luxor. Nos. 3–8 were all penned by the same scribe and were found still tied and sealed with the same seal. Something happened to the courier en route; the letters were never delivered.

The Hermopolis letters are not internally dated, but the script, which is more archaic than that of the Elephantine letters (chaps. 3–4), suggests a date around the end of the sixth century. Some features of the Aramaic are archaic; others are innovative. Still others are reminiscent of a Canaanite language such as Phoenician. This may indicate a scribe not fully conversant with literary Aramaic or may simply reflect a Lower Egyptian regional dialect.

The letters concern family commercial activities. There are frequent references to the purchase and shipment of goods: olive oil, castor oil, perfume, lumber, wool, cloth, leather, and various articles of clothing. Castor oil, produced in the south, had a particularly high trade value. Members of the Memphis branch of the family repeatedly ask their relatives in Syene and Luxor for shipments of it.

Letters 6 and 7 outline a complex financial transaction involving relatives in all three cities. The background can be tentatively reconstructed as follows: Makkebanit, his kinsman Banitsar, and the latter's son are in Memphis; Banitsar's mother, Tabi, is in Luxor; Tashay, Makkebanit's sister, is in Syene. Banitsar and his son have been arrested and imprisoned for debt. Makkebanit has redeemed them; that is, he paid the debt in order to secure their release. In exchange, Banitsar wrote his benefactor an I.O.U. for the amount of the debt. The two letters seek the help of other family members in paying off the debt. Tabi is asked to pay a share of her son's obligation to Makkebanit by sending an equivalent value of wool to Makkebanit's sister in Syene. Makkebanit writes to Tashai in Syene (No. 6) while Banitsar writes his mother in Luxor (No. 7), describing how the transaction is to take place (Porten and Greenfield 1974; Hillers 1979).

The second group of family letters (Nos. 10 and 11) is known as the Padua papyri, after the Civic Museum in Padua, where they are now located. They date from the fifth century, but No. 10 is perhaps a generation older than No. 11. The exact Egyptian provenance of the two letters is not known, though we may conjecture that they were found at Elephantine.

No. 10 was written by one Oshea, a Jewish resident of Migdol in the eastern Delta, to his son Shelomam, who is traveling in Upper Egypt. The letter was dispatched to Elephantine, to be held for the son's arrival. Apparently Shelomam is entitled to a government salary, perhaps because he and his associates are soldiers assigned to caravan escort duty (Porten 1968: 42). The local government office at Migdol has refused to pay Shelomam's salary while he is away, and Oshea has evidently arranged to have the money held until the young man gets back. The damaged middle of the letter alludes to some household misfortune. Oshea informs his son that it is not serious and that Shelomam should not be overly upset by it. The final section reports on several articles of clothing destined for various family members.

No. 11 is a fragment of a letter written by a young man to an older woman. He mentions a lawsuit involving a certain Pakhnum and urges his correspondent to give money to this person, but the details are lost. The letter concludes with personal greetings.

In these letters there is considerable ambiguity in the use of familial designations such as "mother," "sister," and "brother." Sometimes the words have their ordinary meaning. At other times they are used as honorific or generic titles to address relatives, but without intending to specify the actual relationship. A case in point is No. 9, whose initial address "to my mother Atardimri from your brother Ami," would be nonsense if taken literally. On the outside address of this letter, Ami refers to the same woman as "my sister." Similarly, No. 10 is addressed "to my son Shelomam from your brother Oshea" (outside address: "to my brother Shelomam son of Oshea from your brother Oshea"). In No. 7, we find Tabi addressed as Banitsar's "mother" in the outside address, but as his "sister" in the letter proper. No. 11 uses "mother–son" language in the greeting, but a different woman, Menahemet, is identified by the writer as "my mother" in line 5. "Mama" (Nos. 4–5) is a personal name or nickname.

Further confusion is introduced by the occasional practice of using alternative name forms for the same person, for example, Nabushezib-Nabusha (No. 5; cf. Nos. 6 and 7), Atardimri-Atardi (No. 9). Another kind of ambiguity occurs where the formal terms "your servant" and "my lord" are used among family members, as in No. 4. Frequently it is unclear whether the language of family relationship is to be taken literally, and we are unsure of the true relationship of the persons so named. Probably some of the other Aramaic letters also follow this ambiguous practice. In many cases, we are not well enough informed to judge.

Nearly all the letters in this chapter include a distinctive "temple greeting" formula, directed to sanctuaries located where the recipients live. The Hermopolis letters include greetings to temples of Nabu (No. 3), Banit (Nos. 4 and 6), Bethel (No. 5), and "the Queen of Heaven" (No. 5) at Syene. No. 10 has a corresponding greeting to the temple of YHW at Elephantine. In addition, most of the Hermopolis letters (Nos. 3–8) include a blessing in the name of Ptah, the chief divinity of Memphis, where the senders live.

The letters in chaps. 2–5 come from the period when the kings of Persia dominated the ancient Near East. A sketch of this era, focusing on the satrapy of Egypt with which most of the letters are associated, helps place them in their proper setting. Reference is made in other chapters to the satrapies of Abar-Nahara ("across the river"), the huge trans-Euphrates region to which Judah and Samaria belonged, and Babylonia, originally part of a larger district of Mesopotamia and Abar-Nahara, that was made into a separate administrative area by Darius I in 516 B.C.E.

Cyrus the Great (550–530 B.C.E.) was the founder of the Persian empire, known as the "Achaemenid" empire after the name of Achaemenes, the traditional ancestor of the ruling house. Cyrus's reputation rested on his conquests; we know little about how he administered his realm. His son and successor, Cambyses (529–522), brought Egypt into the empire, but he died within a few years during a series of revolts in which various pretenders tried to seize the throne.

Darius I (521–486) had to spend his first two years reestablishing order, as he recounts in his famous trilingual inscription at Behistun. According to Herodotus (*History* 3.90–97), Darius organized the administration of the empire into twenty satrapies, of which Egypt was the sixth. The Behistun inscription lists twenty-two subject lands, not counting Persia itself.

Two-thirds of the way through Darius's reign (499), the Ionian cities in Asia Minor rebelled. There followed a series of altercations with the Greeks, leading up to Darius's unsuccessful invasion of the Greek mainland, which was brought to an abrupt end by the Persian defeat at Marathon (490). On the accession of Darius's son, Xerxes (486–465), a revolt broke out in Egypt that took some three years to put down. After dealing harshly with a second revolt in Babylonia, Xerxes turned his attention back to Greece. The Greek wars, whose details lie beyond our scope, culminated in the Persian calamities at Salamis (480), Platea and Samos (479), and ultimately led to a complete Persian withdrawal from Europe.

Although these events involved Egypt only peripherally, they provide the backdrop for the political instability that was endemic there during the fifth century. Rebellions at the beginning of the reigns of Xerxes and Artaxerxes I (465–424) took years to subdue. In 465, a Libyan named Inaros initiated a revolt, with Athenian support, that almost succeeded. He and his supporters drove the Persian army out of the Delta and placed Memphis under siege before the Persians were able to reestablish control.

Egypt was hardly more stable during the long reign of Darius II (423–404). Insurrections broke out periodically at Elephantine, Thebes, and elsewhere, to which there are repeated allusions in the letters (Nos. 32–34, 40, 42–43; there are hints of tension also in Nos. 31 and 38). Shortly after the beginning of the reign of Artaxerxes II

(404–358), there occurred yet another major revolt in Egypt. This time the Egyptians expelled their Persian suzerains, and they regained independence under native rulers for over half a century, the Twenty-eighth, Twenty-ninth, and Thirtieth Dynasties.

===== **Family Business Letters from Lower Egypt** =====

3. Hermopolis 1 (Cairo Univ., Arch. Mus. P. 1687)
(Late sixth–early fifth century)

A

1   שלם בית נבו אל אחתי רעיה מן אחכי מכבנת

2   ברכתכי לפתח זי יחזני אפיך בשלם שלם בנתסרל ואורי

3   ואסרשת ושרדר חרוץ שאל שלמהן וכעת שלם {ל}}

4   לחרוץ תנה אל תצפי לה כדי תכלן תעבדן לה עבד אנה

5   לה ותפמת ואחתסן מסבלן לה וכעת ארה ספר לה שלחתי

6   בשמה וכעת זי מלתי ˆלבתיˆ לאמר לה שאל על חרוץ כעת

7   {מ} ‹ה› לו כזי עבד אנה לחרוץ כות תעבד בנת עלי

B

8   ארה לא אחי הו חרוץ וכעת הלו יהב להן פרס

9   תנה ויתלקח קדמתהן בסון וכעת הן את ערב עליכי

10 אתיה לתפמת וכעת מדעם אל תזבני בכסת ותשרי לה

11 שלם יקיה הוי שלחת לה וכעת הוי חזית על תשי ועל

12 ברה ושלחי כל טעם זי הוה בב ˆיˆתי לשלמכי שלחת ספר —

13 ה זנה

14 אל אבי פסמי בר נבונתן מן מכבנת סון יבל

Greetings to the temple of Nabu!
To my sister Reia from your brother Makkebanit.
    I bless you by Ptah—may he let me see you again in good health!
    Greetings to Banitsarli, Uri, Isireshut, and Sardur. Haruz sends greetings to them.

Haruz is all right here. Don't worry about him! I am doing everything for him you could do yourself. Tapamut and Ahat-sin are providing for him.

I understand you haven't written him. Why? Is it that you're angry at me? Do you think, "He isn't looking after Haruz?" May Banit do as well for me as I am doing for Haruz! After all, he's my brother, isn't he?

The others have received their salary here, but it can be drawn on at Syene only in their presence. So if any guarantor makes a claim against you, let him bring it to Tapamut. Don't sell the cloak so you can buy something else — don't let it go![1]

Give my best to Yekia. And do look after Tashai and her son. Let me know everything that's happening at home.

I am sending this letter to greet you!

Address: To my father Psami son of Nabunetan from Makkebanit. Let it be carried to Syene.

4. Hermopolis 3 (Cairo Univ., Arch. Mus. P. 1689)
(Late sixth–early fifth century)

A

1 שלם בית בנת בסון על מראי פסמי עבדך מכבנת ברכתך

2 לפתח זי יחזני אפיך בשלם שלם אמי ממה שלם

3 אחי בתי ואנשתה ובנוהי שלם רעיה אל תצף לחרוץ

4 לה שבק אנה לה 1 כדי מטאה ידי וכעת עבד אנה לה

5 אל אחי וחפרע מן אחך מכבנת שלם וחין שלחת לך וכעת

6 הן מטאך סר / חלצה שלח לי ביד עקבה בר וחפרע

7 וכעת כל זי תצבה שלח לי הושר לי משכן

8 מסת לבש משך 1

B

9 והוי לקח שערן מן תשי ויחב בנשרן

10 ושבק כל נשר זי תשכח לממה זבנת חטבת ומשח

11 בשם למתיה לכן ולה אשכחת אש למיתית לכן וכעת

12 תקם יתו לי חפנן 5 אל תצפו לי לכן אנה יצף

13 לשלמכן שלחת {{לן .]} ספרה זנה

14 אל אבי פסמי מן מכבנת בר פסמי סון יבל

Greetings to the temple of Banit at Syene!
To my lord Psami from your servant Makkebanit.
    I bless you by Ptah — may he let me see you again in good health!
    Greetings to my mother Mama. Greetings to my brother Beti, his wife and children.
    Greetings to Reia. Don't let her worry about Haruz. Insofar as possible, I do not leave him alone. I am also providing for him.

To my brother Wahpre from your brother Makkebanit.
    May you live long and well.
    If the *pot of new oil*[2] has reached you, send me word by Akba son of Wahpre. Let me know what you need. Send me enough skins for a leather garment. You should be getting some barley from Tashai. Trade it for lumber and store all the lumber you find at Mama's place.
    I have bought some striped material and scented oil to send to you, but I haven't yet found anyone to bring them. Please have five small measures of castor oil sent to me.
    Don't worry about me; let me worry about you instead! I am sending this letter to greet you.

Address: To my father Psami from Makkebanit son of Psami.
Let it be carried to Syene.

5. Hermopolis 4 (Cairo Univ., Arch. Mus. P. 1690)
(Late sixth–early fifth century)

A

1   שלם בית בתאל ובית מלכת שמין אל אחתי נניחם

2   מן אחכי נבושה ברכתכי לפתח זי יחוני אפיך בשלם

3   שלם ביתאלנתן שלם נכי ועשה ותשי וענתי ואטי ורע׳

4   וכעת מטתני כתנה זי אושרתי לי ואשכחתה שנטת כלה

5   ולבכי לה דבק לה הן חזית מה אתרתן אתגננה בתקבה

6   1 לאטי וכעת כתנה זי התתי לי סון הי מלבש

7   אנה וכעת תקם יתו לן ונתנהי במשח וכעת אל

8   תצפי לן לי ולמכבנת לכן אנחן יצפן אזדהרי

9   בביתאלנתן מן חבב וכעת אן אשכחת אש מהימן

10   אתה לכן מדעם שלם שבתי בר שוג שלם פסי

B

שלם עדר בר פסי שלם שאל בר פטחרטים ואשה 11
בר פטחנם שלם סחתה כלה לשלמכן שלחת ספרה 12
זנה שלם אבי פסמי מן עבדך נבושה שלם אמי 13
ממה }ו{]ו[שלם אחי בתי ואנשתה שלם וחפרע 14
אל נניחם מן נבושזב בר פטחנם סן 15

Greetings to the temple of Bethel and the temple of the Queen of Heaven. To my sister Nanaiham from your brother Nabusha.

I bless you by Ptah—may he let me see you again in good health!

Greetings to Bethelnetan. Greetings to Nikkai(?), Asah, Tashai, Anati, Ati, and Reia.

The tunic you sent me has arrived. I found it all streaked;[3] I just don't like it at all! Do you have plenty of other kinds? If I knew, I would exchange it for a dress[4] for Ati. I do wear the tunic you brought to Syene for me.

Please have some castor oil sent to us, so we can exchange it for olive oil.

Don't worry about me and Makkebanit; let us worry about you instead! Take care of Bethelnetan; keep Habib away from him! If I can find anyone dependable, I will send you something.

Greetings to Shabbetai son of Shug. Greetings to Pasai. Greetings to Eder son of Pasai. Greetings to Sheil son of Petehortais and Asah son of Petekhnum. Greetings to the whole neighborhood.

I am sending this letter to greet you! Greetings to my father Psami from your servant Nabusha. Greetings to my mother Mama. Greetings to my brother Beti and his household. Greetings to Wahpre.

Address: To Nanaiham from Nabushezib son of Petekhnum. To Syene.

6. Hermopolis 2 (Cairo Univ., Arch. Mus. P. 1688)
(Late sixth–early fifth century)

A

שלם בית בנת בסון אל אחתי תשי מן אחכי מכבנת 1
ברדתכי לפתח זי יחזני אפיכי בשלם שלם נבושה 2
תנה אל תצפו לה לה מנם אנה לה מן מפי שלם 3
פסמי יקה שלם נניחם וכעת הלו מסת כספה זי 4

5   הוה בידי נתתן ופדת לבנתסר בר תבי אחת

6   נבושה כסף ש׳ 6 וזוז כסף זוז וכעת שלחי

7   על תבי ותושר לכי עמר מן קצתה זי כסף ש׳ 1

8   וכעת הן יהב לכי נקיה ונזתה שלחי לי

9   והן יהב לכי עמרה זי על מכי שלחי לי

10   והלה יהב לכי שלחי לי ואקבל עליהן תנה

11   וכעת זבנת משח זית ליקה לכתן ואף לכי תקבת

12   1 שפרת ואף משח בשם לבת בנת ולעד אשכח

13   אש למושרתהם לכן וכעת הושרי לי תקם חפנן

14   5 והוי יהבת עבר לוחפרע ויהוי זבן נשרן

15   ושבק בבתה אל תקמי קדמתה כל נשר זי ישכח

16   יזבן והן יהב לכי רעיה עמר שלחי לי שלם

17   תטסרי אזדהרי בה לשלמכן שלחת ספרה זנה

B

18   אל תשי מן מכבנת בר פסמי סון יבל

Greetings to the temple of Banit at Syene!
To my sister Tashai from your brother Makkebanit.

I bless you by Ptah—may he let me see you again in good health!

Nabusha is well here. Do not worry about him. I am not taking him away from Memphis. Greetings to Psami and Yake. Greetings to Nanaiham.

The sum of money I had—I have paid it to redeem Banitsar,[5] the son of Nabusha's sister Tabi: 6½ silver shekels at the usual rate of conversion.[6] Tell Tabi to send you one shekel's worth of wool as her share of the money. If you are given a lamb to shear, let me know. If you are given the wool owed to me(?), let me know. And if you are not given anything, let me know so I can register a complaint against them here.

I have bought some olive oil and a tunic for Yakeh, a pretty dress(?) for you, and some scented oil for the temple of Banit. But I still haven't found anyone to bring them to you.

Send me five small measures of castor oil. And give some grain to Wahpre. He will be buying lumber and storing it at his house. Don't get in his way— let him buy all the lumber he can find!

If Reia has sold you any wool, let me know.

Greetings to Tetosiri. Take good care of her! I am sending this letter to greet you.

Address: To Tashai from Makkebanit son of Psami.
Let it be carried to Syene.

7. Hermopolis 6 (Cairo Univ., Arch. Mus. P. 1692)
(Late sixth–early fifth century)

A

1   אל אחתי תבי מן אॵ]חוכי בנתסן]ר ברכתכי לפתח זי

2   יחוני אפיכי בשן]לם ואף . . . . בן]רי שאל שלמכי

3   וכעת יהב מן]כבנת בר פסמי]חתנה זי נבשה כסף

4   ש' 6 וזז כ]סף זז ואזל]ואפקני אנה וברי

5   וכתבת לה ען]לה ספרה אזלי]וזבני עמר כזי תמט–

6   ה ידכי ואו]שריהי לתשי ס]ון הלו כספה זי הוה

7   בידה יהב ען]לי ל . . . . נבשה ומכ]בנת שאלן שלמכי

B

8   ושלם תרו מ̇ן] אחוכי מכבנת וכ]עת שלם בנתסר תנה

9   וברה אל תן]צפי לה וכעת הלו]אנחן בען אלף

10   ויתונה לכן לן]שלמכי שלחת ס]פרה זנה

11   אל אמי]תבי מן בנתסר בר] סרה אפי יבל

To my sister Tabi from [your brother Banitsar].
I bless you by Ptah—may he let me see you again in good health!
My son [. . .] sends greetings to you.
[Makkebanit son of Psami], Nabusha's son-in-law, paid 6½ silver shekels (at the usual rate of conversion) [and god] me released—my son and I—and I wrote him [a document of obligation for it. Go] buy as much wool as you can and send [it to Tashai at] Syene. He paid my [debt to . . .] with the sum of money he had.
[Nabusha and] Makkebanit send greetings to you and Taru.
[A postscript from your brother Makkebanit:] Banitsar is well here. As for his son—don't [worry about him.] We are trying to find a boat to send him back on.
I am sending this letter to greet you!

Address: To my mother [Tabi from Banitsar son of] Sarah.
Let it be carried to Luxor.

8. Hermopolis 5 (Cairo Univ., Arch. Mus. P. 1691)
(Late sixth–early fifth century)

A

1 אל אחתי תרו ותבי מן אחוכן נבושה ומכבנת ברכנכן
2 לפתח זי יחזני אפיכן בשלם וכעת תדען זי מדעם
3 לה מפקן לן מן סון ואף מן זי נפקת מן סון שאל
4 לה הושר לי ספר ומנדעם וכעת יהתו לן ארון
5 וביננבן והן תכלן תהיתן לן תקם יתו ביד חרוץ
6 בר ביתאלשזב זי אתה למחתה לבמרשרי אתריה
7 ומהי דה זי ספר לה הושרתן

B

8 לי ואנה נכתני חויה והות מית ולה שלחתן
9 הן חי אנה והן מת אנה לשלמכן שלחת ספרה זנה
10 אל תרו מן נבושה בר פטחנם אפי יבל

To my sisters Taru and Tabi from your brother Nabusha (and Makkebanit). We bless you by Ptah—may he let us see you again in good health!

You should know that they aren't sending us anything from Syene. Sheil hasn't sent me a letter or anything else!

They should ship us a chest and a plank of . . .-wood. If you can send us some castor oil, do so by Haruz son of Bethelshezeb, who is going to bring the military officials[7] to . . . .

What's wrong? Why haven't you sent me a letter? Even when I nearly died of snakebite, you didn't write to see whether I was alive or dead!

I am sending this letter to greet you!

Address: To Taru from Nabusha son of Petekhnum.
Let it be carried to Luxor.

9. Hermopolis 7 (Cairo Univ., Arch. Mus. P. 1693)
(Late sixth–early fifth century)

A

1   אל אמי עתרדמרי מן אחוכי אמי שֻׁ]לם ו]חין שלחת לכי

2   שלם אחתי אסורי וזבבו וכבי וכען עליכי מתכל אנה הוי

3   חזית על ינקיא אלכי שלם וסרז ושפנית ובניה ופטממון שלם

4   הריוטא ואחתהה לשלמכי שלחת ספרא זנה

B

5   אל אחתי עתרדי מן אֹחֹו]נכי א]מֹי אפי יובל

To my mother Atardimri from your brother Ami.
May you live [well] and long.
Greetings to my sister Isiwere and Zababu and Kake. I am trusting you to look after those children! Greetings to Vasaraza, and Shepeneith and her children, and Peteamun. Greetings to Haryuta and her sister.
I am sending this letter to greet you!

Address: To my sister Atardi from your brother Ami.
Let it be carried to Luxor.

===== **To a Son on a Journey** =====

10. Padua 1 (Museo Civico di Padova)
(Provenance unknown, ca. 475–450)

A

1   שלם ב]ית יהו ציב אל ברי שלמם [מ]ן אחוך אושע שלם ושררת
    הושרת לך]

2   [וכעת] מן יום זי אזלת בארחא זך לבבי לא טיב אף אמך כעת ברך
    אנת [ליהו אלהא]

3   [זי יח]וני אנפיך בשלם כעת מן יום זי נפקתם מן מצרין פרם לא
[ינ]היב לן תנה]

4   [וכזי] קבלן לפחותא על פרסכן תנה במגדל כן אמיר לן לאמר על זנה
[אנתם קבלו]

5   [קדם] ספריא ויתיהב לכן כעת כזי תאתון מצרין
[. . . . על]

6   [. . פ]רסכן זי כלי כלה כעת איך ביתא עביד ואיך נפקת הן
[. . . . . יהון]

7   [. . . . ש]לם ומחבל לא איתי גבר הוי אל תתאשד עד תאתה
[. . . . .]

B

[. . . . .]   8

9   [כזי כתבת] באגרתא זילך על כתון ולבש כתונך ולבשך עבידן
[. . . . .]

10   [. . . .] לאמך עבדת אל תמלי לבת כזי לא איתית המו מנפי כזי תנ]אתה
תמה]

11   [איתין] המו קדמתך כעת זבנת לי אנה כֹתן 1   זי כתן כעת
[. . . . .]

12   [. . . . כ]ן ולבש עד תאתה שלם אמך וינקיא כלא כעת תנה הוין
[. . . . .]

13   [ב . . .] למחר כתבת אגרתא זא כזי כן שמיע לן לאמר תתפטרן
[. . . . .]

14   אל אחי שלמם בר אﬠﬡ[ן]שע אחוך אושע בר פטﬥ[. . . . . . .]

Greetings to the temple of YHW in Elephantine!
To my son Shelomam from your brother Oshea.

I send you greetings and wishes for your good health.

Since you left on your trip, my mind has not been at ease. Neither has your mother's. I pray that [the God YHW] will bless you, and let me [see] you again in good health.

Since you left Lower Egypt, we have not been [paid] your salary [here]. When we complained about your salary to the government officials here in

Migdol, they told us, "[You should complain] about this [to] the bookkeepers, and it will be paid to you." So when you come back to Lower Egypt, [*you will be able to receive*] your salary which was withheld.

How is the household doing, and how was your departure? If [. . .] will be [. . .] well, and no damage was done. Be a man! Don't cry(?) until you come [. . .].

[You wrote] in your letter about a tunic and a garment. They have been made. [. . .] I have made for your mother. Don't be angry that I haven't brought them to Memphis. When you [come there, I will bring] them to you.

I have bought myself a linen tunic, [. . .] and a garment until you come.

Your mother and all the children are fine. We are [. . .] here. [On the . . .] of Mehir I wrote this letter[8] when we got word that you would be released [. . .].

Address: To my brother Shelomam son of Oshea from your brother Oshea son of Pet[. . .].

A Son to His Mother

11. Padua 2 (Museo Civico di Padova)
(Provenance unknown, ca. 425–400 B.C.E.)

A

1   אל אמ[ין] יהוישמע ברך שלום [שלם ושררת שניא הושרת]

2   לך שלם גלגל תנה שלם ינקיה ונ[כ]ע̇נ[ת] זך [. . . . . . .]

3   זילי הבה לפחנום בר נבודלה ויעבנך . . . . [

4   ינרוהי והן איתי כסף הבי עלוהי [. . . . .] לשלמכ[י]ן

5   שלחת ספרה זנה שלם ^אמי^ מנחמת שלם [. . . . .] שלם[

6   יהוישמע

B

7   [אל אמ]י̇ יהו̇ישמ̇ע בר̇[ת . . . .]

To my mother Yahuyishma from your son Shallum.
[I send] you greetings and best wishes for your good health.

Galgul is well here. Greetings to the children.

That [. . .] of mine, give it to Pakhnum son of Nabudelah so he can make [. . .]. [. . .] they will sue him. If there is any money, give it to him. [. . .].

I am writing to [greet you]. Greetings to my mother Menahemet, [to . . . and to] Yahuyishma.

Address: [To] my [mother] Yahuyishma daughter of [. . .].

Notes

1. The Aramaic is unclear. I understand the literal sense to be, "Do not buy (anything) with the garment, or release it!"
2. For the translation, see Grelot 1972: 158 and n. e.
3. Or "frayed, ripped." See Grelot 1972: 160a; Gibson 1975: 138.
4. Or "pot." The same word, with a slightly different spelling, appears in No. 6.
5. An alternative reading yields, "I have invested it at interest with Banitsar."
6. Literally, "six silver shekels and a *zuz,* at one silver *zuz* (to the ten)." See the glossary (*karsh*) on this expression.
7. Literally, "Assyrians"(?). The meaning of the Aramaic word is uncertain, but it is possibly found again in No. 18. The name of the place to which they are to be delivered cannot be identified.
8. Or "[. . .] tomorrow. I wrote this letter. . . ."

III

Ostraca from Elephantine

Introduction

All but one of the letters in this chapter were found at the beginning of the twentieth century C.E. on the island of Elephantine in Upper Egypt. The exception, No. 17, was found at Aswan (ancient Syene), on the east bank of the Nile facing Elephantine. All of them date to around 475 B.C.E. In fact, though various senders are identified by name, the letters appear to have been written by the same hand, probably a self-employed public scribe or a moonlighting government employee (Naveh 1970: 37–38; cf. Wente 1990: 8–9). Persons in Syene wishing to send a message to family or business associates on the island had only to go to the scribe and dictate their message. A short communication would be written on an ostracon and put into the hands of the next boatman crossing over to the island, where it would be passed on to the addressee.

These letters show few of the formal marks of proper epistolary style. They are often cryptic. Friends and relatives who have seen one another only a few hours or a few days previously have no need to explain matters of common knowledge. While these letters do not speak of great events that would attract the interest of the political or military historian, they provide glimpses into the everyday life of the residents of this small and close-knit community.

The subject matter is varied: an ominous dream (No. 12), the payment of debts including one owed to a religious organization (No. 13), livestock (Nos. 15 and 17), foodstuffs, clothing and other common commodities. A cryptic but intriguing note (No. 21) refers to a garment left in the temple of YHH, possibly for sacral use.

A longer and rather difficult letter (No. 18) deals with slaves. The first part refers to the shipment of slaves. The second half, possibly a separate letter, relates to a transaction in which a female slave-artisan, an Egyptian weaver named Tetosiri, is being leased by her owner to two other persons in succession, one of whom is the writer.

37

Two letters allude to Jewish religious observances. The writer of No. 20 urges his correspondent to get down to the docks early the next day to receive a shipment of vegetables, so they can be unloaded before the Sabbath begins. In No. 19, a friend or relative of a Jewish family living on the island asks casually, "Let me know when you will be celebrating Passover." Clearly Passover was already being observed at Elephantine half a century before the so-called "Passover papyrus" (No. 30; 419 B.C.E.). Whether the writer's request reflects a time when Passover had no fixed date or whether other factors lie behind it (a delay because of ritual impurity or a possible intercalary month) cannot be determined.

For the general historical background to these letters, see the introduction to chapter II above.

=== **A Dream and Family Matters** ===

12. Berlin, St. Mus. 1137
(Ca. 475 B.C.E.)

A

1   כען הלו חלם
2   חזית ומן
3   עדנא הו אנה
4   חמם שנא
5   ‑תחזי יח
6   מליה
7   שלמ֯י֯‎

B

8   כען הן צבתי
9   אל תזבני / המו
10   יאכלו ינקיא
11   הלו לא
12   שאר
13   קטין

I have had a dream, and since then I have been very feverish. See Yahmolyah and pay him![1]

If you wish, do not sell them.[2] Let the babies eat! There isn't anything left, not even a little bit!

Money for a Religious Society

13. O. Cairo 35468a
(Ca. 475 B.C.E.)

1 עַל חגי אמרת
2 לאשין על כסף
3 מרזחא כן אמר
4 לי לם לאיתו
5 כען אנתננה
6 לחגי או
7 יגדל דבר
8 עלוהי
9 וינתנהי
10 לכם

To Haggai:

I talked to Ashina about the money for the *marzeah* society. He told me [i.e., Ito], "I will give it to Haggai or to Yigdal." So go see him, and get him to give it to you!

A Report of Imprisonment

14. O. Clermont-Ganneau 44
(Ca. 475 B.C.E.)

A

1 שלם ידניה כען לו
2 [במ]סנרא שימת ופקיד

3 [אמר לם י]כֹלאו מנה לחם ומין

4 [. . . . .] לי אחוטב להן

5 [. . . . .] יֹֹ]וֹם שבה

B

6 כען הן לא שֹבו לנתן תמה

7 ינפק אלי ואהך אגרם [. . . .]

8 עֹא אף הושרו לי לֹן[. . . . .]

9 ואכתבֹ [. . . . .]

10 וֹאֹלֹ [. . . . . .]

Greetings, Yedanyah!

She has been put in jail, and orders have been given that she is not to be provided with bread and water.

[. . .] Ahutab has [. . .] to me, except [. . .] the Sabbath day.

If Natan has not been taken captive there, let him come over to where I am, so I can go grind [meal(?)]. Also send me [. . .], and I will write [. . .]. Do not(?) [. . .].

================ **Sheepshearing** ================

15. Berlin, St. Mus. 11383
(Ca. 475 B.C.E.)

A

1 שלם אוריה כען

2 הלו תאתא זילך

3 רבתא מטאת למנז

4 עמרא זילה קדמא

5 מתמרט בכבא כען

6 אתא ונזה ביום

7 תרחֹמֹנה

8 תגזנה

B

9 והן לא תנפק
10 יומא זנה שלח
11 לי וארחעה עד
12a תנפק

Greetings, Uriyah!
Your big ewe is ready now for shearing. The one you sent over before is
being combed now. You can come shear her whenever you please. If you aren't
going to come today, let me know and I will wash her before you come over.

═══════════════ **Bread and Flour** ═══════════════

16. Berlin, St. Mus. 11383
(Ca. 475 B.C.E.)

12b שלם אחטב
13 כען על לחמא זנה
14 אכל עד מחר
15 ע]רובה א׳ / קמח
16 שאר תנה

Greetings, Ahutab!
About this bread—eat it until tomorrow (Friday).[3] There is still an *ardab*
of flour left here.

===== Sheep Marketing =====

17. Cambridge 131–133
(Aswan, ca. 475 B.C.E.)

A

1   [א]ל֯ אמי קווליה ברכנ֯י . . . . שלם]

2   שלחת לכי כענת הלו הו[ן]דעתכי]

3   נפנא רעיא ˆקן ˆ זי סחמרי בעל

4   טבתכם אתה סון עם קנה

5   לוּבנה אזלי קומי

6   עמה בסון יומא

7   זנה הן תעבדן

B

8   [. . . . .] ל[ה בסון יעבד לי

9   [תנה כ]ן הלו גזר לי לם אזל

10   [לבי]ן֯תי ויִנתנו לחנה ענז 1 עד

11   תמטאנך כען חזרו ו[. . . .]

12   למעבד לה הלו מנין המו

13   אף לחם אף קמח הו

14   [את]ה ושאלהי

15   לם מה תבעי

To my mother Qawwileyah from your son [. . .].

I send you greetings!

This is to let you know that your partner Nefna, the shepherd from Sahmeri, has come to Syene with sheep to sell. Come over to Syene today to help him. If you will do [this for] him in Syene, he will do something for me here. He promised(?) me, "Come to my house and they will give you a goat for Hannah before she arrives where you are."

They went back and [*were not able*] to do it. They are taking inventory of bread and flour. But now he has come. You ask him, "What do you want us to do?"

Money and Slaves

18. Bodleian Aram. Inscr. 1 (Lost)
(Ca. 475 B.C.E.)

A

1 כענת]חזי . . . . . [הוֹשֵׁרוֹהִי
2 למל]כי[ה מפֹּי למכתבה אף כזֹי
3 תשמעון לאמר אֹשׂריֹא יהבן פרם
4 בסון שלחֹא עלי חזי נחת קפירא
5 זי היתת ביב הושרוהי לי וקפרא זי
6 הושרת לכֹם מֹן]. .[יֹרא
7 וקפירא רבא זי יהב
8 לֹם מלכיה הושרוֹ-
9 הם לה

B

10 כענת חזו חנתא זי יהב לי אוריה לנסכא
11 הביה לנגמריה בר אחיו ויערכה מן
12 שכרא ובלוה לאוריא אן חזי תטוסרי
13 הֹלֹן יכתבוה על דרעה עלא מן כתבתא
14 זֹי על דרעה הלו כן שלח לאמר זי
15 לא ישכחן עלימתה
16 מ ‹ת› כתבה על
17 שמה

[See to . . .]. Have him sent to Malkiyah at Memphis to be inscribed.

Also, when you hear that the officials[4] are making salary payments at Syene, let me know.

See to Nakht, the slave[5] I brought to Elephantine—have him sent to me. The slave I sent to you from [. . .], and the big slave(?) Malkiyah gave me— have them sent to him.

See to the slave-girl[6] Uriyah gave me for the weaving. Give her to Gemaryah son of Ahyo and let him determine her wages[7] and send her back[8] to Uriyah.

And see to Tetosiri herself. Have her marked on the arm with "*hln*"[9] above the mark that is already there. Uriyah has written me that he had better not find his servant-girl marked with his (Gemaryah's?) name.

════════════════ **Family Messages: Passover** ════════════════

19. Bodleian Aram. Inscr. 7
(Ca. 475 B.C.E.)

A

1   אל הושעיה

2   שלמך כען חזי

3   על / ינקיא עד תאת-

4   ה אחטב אל תוכ-

5   ל המו על אחרנן

B

6   הן גרסו לחמהם

7   לשו לחם קב 1   עד

8   תאתה אמהם שלח

9   לי אמת תעבדן פסח-

10   א הוי שלח שלם

11   ינקא

To Hoshayah: Greetings!

Take care of the children until Ahutab gets there. Don't trust anyone else with them!

If the flour for your bread has been ground, make up a small portion of dough to last until their mother gets there.

Let me know when you will be celebrating Passover.

Tell me how the baby is doing!

════════════ **Repair of a Garment** ════════════

20. O. Clermont-Ganneau 70
(Ca. 475 B.C.E.)

A

1   אל מרי מיכיה עבדך

2   גדל שלם וחין שלחת

3   לך ברכתך ליהה ולחנ[נב]

4   כען שלח / לי לבשא

B

5   זי עליך ויחטנה

6   לשלמך שלחת ספרֹא

To my lord Mikayah, from your servant Gaddul.
  May you live long and well! I bless you by YHH and Khnum.
  Send me the garment you have on.[10] so it can be re-stitched. I am writing to greet you.

════════════ **Dedication of a Tunic** ════════════

21. O. Cairo 49624
(Ca. 475 B.C.E.)

1   חזו כתוני זי

2   שבקת בית [בית]

3   יהה אמרי לאריה

4   [י]חרמה   על סלואה

Look after the tunic I left in the temple of YHH. Tell Uriyah it is to be dedicated.

Address: To Salluah.

Handling of Produce and the Sabbath

22. O. Clermont-Ganneau 152
(Ca. 475 B.C.E.)

A

1   שלם יסלח כענת הא בקלא אוש-

2   ר מחר ערקי אלפא מחר בשבה

3   למה הן יאבד חי / ליהה הן לא נפשכ[ין]

4   אלקח אל תתכלי על משלמת

5   ועל שמעיה כען החלפי לי שער̇[ן]̇

6   [{] בעי פרא חט המו בקט כענת

7   חי / ליהה הן לא על

8   נפשכי

B

9   [חשב]נה על דבר תקבר מה זי

10 הושרת תחת חמר להו[ן]ם כל[א]

11 הושרתה הן משלמת לא מצֿאת

12 לי אנתי מה תאמרן תחזין אנפי

13 ואחזה אפיכי

Greetings, Yislah!

Look, I'm sending you the vegetables tomorrow. Get there before the boat comes in — on account of the Sabbath — so they won't be spoiled. I swear to God, if you don't, I'll kill you! Don't trust Meshullemet or Shemayah to take care of it.

Trade the barley for me. Try to get a lamb[11]. . . . I swear to God, if you don't, you'll have to pay the bill yourself!

As for the . . . you sent in exchange for the wine, I have sent it all on to them(?). If Meshullemet doesn't get here, what will you say?

May we see each other soon!

Shopping Lists and Shipping Orders

23. O. Clermont-Ganneau 16
(Ca. 475 B.C.E.)

A

1   הושרו / לי
2   מלח קבן 2
3   דקק וחצף
4   קפתא עלוהי
5   אף הזי

B

6   אפק לי תלי
7   וכתון 1 הן
8   יעדרן ותפק
9   אחטב / עמֹר
10 1 פול / פֹּל-
11 חֹ

Send me two *qab*s of salt, fine and coarse grade. The basket is to put it in. Also, send me a pickaxe and a tunic; there is hoeing[12] to do. Have Ahutab send over an *omer* of cut beans.

24. O. Clermont-Ganneau 169
(Ca. 475 B.C.E.)

A

1   [ש]לם אחוטב כען הושרי
2   לי זעיר מלח יומא זנה
3   והן מלח לאית בביתא

4 זבנו מן אלפי עבורא

5 זי ביב הלו

6 לאיתי לי

B

7 מלח למשם בקמח נ] . . [ת

Greetings, Ahutab!
Send me some salt right away—today! If there isn't any salt in the house,
then buy some from Alpay the ferryman[13] at Elephantine. I don't have any
salt left to put in the flour [. . .].

25. O. Clermont-Ganneau 228
(Ca. 475 B.C.E.)

A

1 מן מיכיה על א]חוטב[

2 שלמכי כענת חזי]נפותא[

3 רבתא ואף זעירתא]לקמח[

4 אל ינפי מנהם הלו

5 שנא זי לא

B

6]עבדו ב]הם חזי עקא זי

7]הושר]ת לכי ביד פמן הבהי

8] . . . .[שרי אף בעי גלדא

9]זי [אמרת לכי הלו עליכי

10 הו אל יאבד

From Mikayah to [Ahutab].
Greetings to you!
See to the large [sieve] and the small one [for the flour]. Don't let it be sifted
without them.[14] There is a lot that hasn't been [. . .].
See to the lumber I [had] Pamin [bring you]. Give it to [. . .].
Would you also ask for the skin I told you about? It's charged to you, so
don't let anything happen to it!

26. O. Clermont-Ganneau 186
(Ca. 475 B.C.E.)

A

1 ‏יה שלמך יהה[. . . . . .]
2 ‏[צבאת ישא]ל בכל עדן כען כזי
3 ‏זי וחפרע בר [. . . . . .]
4 ‏. . . תאת]ה הושר לי
5 ‏. . . .] וכב]שה ומלח
6 ‏[. . . . .]ל

B

7 ‏עד יום שבה]הושרת לך[
8 ‏ביד משלם נונן [. . .] . . . . .]
9 ‏ביד בעדי 3 רכר]בן . . . .]
10 ‏ויהבת לה י]ומא זנה . . .]
11 ‏גזירה [. . . . . .].
12 ‏[. . . . .]

To [. . .]yah: Greetings!
May YHH [of hosts] bless you at all times.
When the [*shipment*] of Wahpre son of [. . .] arrives, send me [. . .] and a lamb(?), and some salt [. . .] before the Sabbath.
[I am having] Meshullam [bring you] some fish [. . .], and [having] Beadi [bring] three big(?) [. . .]. I am giving it to him today [. . .] cut up(?) [. . .].

27. O. Cairo 35468b
(Ca. 475 B.C.E.)

A

1 ‏הושר לי שערן
2 ‏קב 1 וש‹ל›ח / ליוטב
3 ‏כסא זעירא

B

[. . . . . .] 4

[. . . .] . . ל.תה 5

אֹטר אזל תה . . . [. . . .] 6

[. . . . . .] 7

תא[. . . .] 8

[. . . .] 9

    Send me one *qab* of barley, and send Yotab the little cup. [*The rest is illegible.*]

─────────── **Miscellaneous** ───────────

    The two sides of this ostracon bear two different letters (cf. Nos. 15 and 16, also written on the same sherd). The writers of Nos. 28 and 29 are different, but the recipient is the same in both cases. It is not clear whether the two letters are related.

28. BM 45035
(Ca. 475 B.C.E.)

A

שלם מיכיה מן נתן בר גמריה 1

כען אתה על מחר ולא כשרן 2

הלו שכד הו לי למדֹד 3

כען אל תושר למאתה 4

מֹחר 5

    Greetings, Mikayah! From Natan son of Gemaryah.

    He is planning to come tomorrow, but they are not ready(?). I am the one hired to do the measuring![15] So don't send him over tomorrow!

29. BM 45035
(Ca. 475 B.C.E.)

B

שלם מיכיה מן ידניה כענת 6

הֵלוֹ שֵׁלחת לך אתמל בשם 7

הודויה בר זֹכֹריה לם 8

אתה ליומא זנה ולא 9

אתית ביד בנתין [֗]לן [֗.] 10

Greetings, Mikayah! From Yedanyah.

I wrote you yesterday concerning Hodawyah son of Zekaryah, as follows: "He is coming today." But I am not having Banit—[. . .] bring him.

Notes

1. I follow Dupont-Sommer 1948a: 109–30. The widely accepted alternative "I saw an apparition, and it said, 'Peace' or 'All is well'" (Levine 1964: 19; Donner-Röllig 1964–68: 2:321; and Grelot 1972: 21) cannot be reconciled with the characters written on the sherd.

2. Or "do not buy them."

3. The word *ʿrwbh* in later Jewish Aramaic is a special term meaning "day of preparation" (for Sabbath, Passover, or another religious festival). In this later usage, Sabbath eve (i.e., "Friday") is usually meant unless another festival is specified. This technical usage is otherwise attested only in much later texts, however; and the phrase should perhaps be translated simply, "until tomorrow evening."

4. Literally, "Assyrians(?)." The reading is uncertain, but it is perhaps a popular term for officials in the military administration. Text No. 8 may show this same usage.

5. The word *qpyrʾ*, found three times in this text is unexplained; "slave" is a conjecture based on contect.

6. This word is obscure. See Lindenberger 1984: 53; "Slave-Girl."

7. This refers to a sum paid to the correspondent as middleman, or to wages paid to the slave, which was normally done elsewhere in the Persian empire at this time (Dandamaev 1984b: 120–21).

8. Alternatively, "her fee," to be paid to Uriah, the owner.

9. Slaves were often marked with the names of their owners. The meaning of the mark referred to here is unknown.

10. Or possibly "the garment you have on account."

11. Or "some bran." The following phrase is unintelligible.

12. Or "Send me a plow and a tunic; there is plowing. . . ."

13. Or "from the grain-boats, transport-boats."

14. Or "See to the large [winnowing fan] and the small one [for the wheat]. Do not let it be winnowed without them."

15. "Measuring may refer to taking inventory of supplies (as in No. 17) or possibly to surveying. A third possibility is that the word refers to tailoring clothes. See No. 20.

IV

Archives of the Jewish Community at Elephantine

Introduction

The six papyrus letters in this chapter date to a twelve-year period in the last quarter of the fifth century B.C.E. Discovered at Elephantine in 1907 by archaeologists from the Berlin Museum, they belong to the archives of one man: Yedanyah bar Gemaryah, a leader of the Elephantine Jewish community. Nos. 30 and 31 are addressed to him and his associates, and No. 35 is a memorandum of a message probably delivered to him orally. Nos. 34 and 36 are his letters or preparatory drafts, and he is probably the unnamed author of No. 33. No. 32 relates to his arrest at Thebes. The letters deal with the community's social and religious life and reflect the instability that characterized Upper Egypt during the waning days of Persian control. (See the introduction to chapter 2.)

No. 30, unquestionably the most important letter in this volume for Jewish religious history, is a damaged royal order concerning religious observance. Although it has long been known as the "Passover papyrus" (Sachau 1911: 36–40), the word "Passover" does not occur in the extant fragments. Dated 419 B.C.E., it is addressed to Yedanyah and the other community leaders from "your brother Hananyah," a Jew who was not resident in Elephantine.

Hananyah appears to hold a senior position in the Persian administration in Egypt. He may have been a kind of "minister of state for Jewish affairs," with authority like that exercised by Ezra in Judah and the surrounding region. Whether he is to be identified with "Hanani," the brother of the biblical Nehemiah (Neh 1:2; 7:2) is a much-debated question.

Hananyah begins by stating that he is acting on the authority of Arshama, the Persian satrap of Egypt, who had in turn received his orders from the king. (See the introduction to chapter 5.) Greeting Yedanyah and his colleagues with a stereotyped blessing in the name of "the gods"— an incongruous but not unparalleled note in Jewish correspondence — Hananyah sets forth precise commands concerning the celebration of the feast of Unleavened Bread.

Much of the text is irretrievably lost, and what remains is perplexing. Some provisions are like those found in the Pentateuch: "do not [eat] anything leavened" (Exod 12:15, 19; 13:7; Deut 16:3–4; cf. Exod 23:18; 34:25); the reference to a week of eating unleavened bread (Exod 12:15, 18–19; 13:6–7; 23:15; 34:18; Lev 23:6; Deut 16:3–4, cf. 8; only Exodus 12 uses both the words "fourteenth" and "twenty-first," cf. Lev 23:5); the injunction against work (Exod 12:16; Lev 23:7–8; Deut 16:8); and the association of sunset with the feast of Unleavened Bread (Exod 12:18; contrast Deut 16:6; Exod 12:6, 18; and Lev 23:5, which speak of sundown or evening in connection with Passover).

Other features do not resemble the Pentateuch, especially the command to "bring into your chambers [. . .] and seal." The missing words can hardly refer to anything except leaven, but no such command is known in the Bible or in postbiblical Jewish literature. On the contrary, leaven is supposed to be *removed* from the house; it was ordinarily burned, never stored under seal. Nor is an injunction against drinking (presumably anything made from fermented grain) found in the Bible, though it is taken for granted in the Mishna (*m. Pesah* 3:1; etc.). The exhortation to "be pure" is paralleled only in Ezra 6:20, where it refers to the priests sacrificing the Passover lamb.

The reason for sending the letter cannot have been to introduce the celebration of Passover at Elephantine; the festival is mentioned in letters from half a century earlier (see No. 19 and other fragmentary ostraca from the same period). Was it to link Passover and Unleavened Bread (originally two separate festivals)? Was it to establish a fixed date for Unleavened Bread or a combined festival? The uncertainty about the date of Passover intimated in No. 19 gives this suggestion plausibility. Was it to bring the celebration of Passover at Elephantine into line with its celebration in Jerusalem? It is difficult to imagine the postexilic priestly establishment in Jerusalem allowing the Passover sacrifice to be offered in Egypt. The provisions of Deuteronomy 16 centralizing the Passover in "the place which Yʜwʜ your God will choose" can, however, be interpreted as applying only to Jews residing within the Israelite homeland. The closest biblical parallels to the letter occur not in Deuteronomy but in Exodus 12, a chapter conventionally attributed to the Priestly source but containing components of uncertain age. One scholar suggests a more Machiavellian interpretation — that Hananyah's intent was to warn the Elephantine community of an impending visit by a government inspector, urging them to *appear* to be acting in conformity with the regulations approved in Jerusalem (Smith 1984: 231).

To avoid prejudicing the matter and to make clear the great uncertainty surrounding the interpretation of this letter, I have followed the precedent of A. Vincent (1937: 237–38) by offering the reader two versions: the first based only on the surviving text (No. 30a), with no reconstructions except the completion of common formulas, and the second with extensive reconstructions based on biblical parallels (No. 30b, following the restorations of Porten and Yardeni 1986).

The other letters in the chapter are to be placed a little over a decade later and reflect the deteriorating relations among Jews and Egyptians at Elephantine. No. 31 is addressed to Yedanyah and his colleagues from Mauzyah bar Natan, another well-known leader of the community. Mauzyah has just been released from jail in Abydos, where he had been imprisoned on a spurious charge of theft. Two Egyptians, Seha and Hor, were instrumental in gaining his release and are now on their way to Elephantine. The conclusion of the letter has usually been read as a commendation of the two men. I believe, however, that it is better interpreted as a warning from Mauzyah that despite their having helped him, they are up to no good. No. 32 speaks of riots and looting at Elephantine, naming several men and women arrested there and at Thebes. Some of the names are Jewish, some Egyptian, and some of uncertain affiliation. The letter is not dated.

The four remaining letters concern the most traumatic incident in the history of the Jews of Elephantine: the razing of their temple in 410 B.C.E. No. 33 sets the stage. Written to a Persian official whose name is lost, it accuses the Egyptian priests of bribing Vidranga, the corrupt district governor, and then running riot in the Jewish quarter of the island, stopping up a well and building a wall in the middle of the fortress. The writers demand a hearing before the regional judiciary, so that blame can be apportioned. The fragmentary conclusion alludes to vandalism in the temple and requests an injunction to prevent any such incidents in the future.

No. 34 describes the actual destruction of the temple, which took place shortly afterwards. This letter is extant in two copies, with slight textual differences. "Text A," evidently a preliminary draft, is complete and has been taken as the primary basis for the translation, although the more fragmentary "Text B" is probably closer to the version actually sent. Addressed to the governor of Judah from Yedanyah on behalf of the entire community, No. 34 is a formal petition for permission to rebuild the temple and reinstitute sacrifice. Written three years after the events, it narrates in vivid detail what happened in 410. With the collusion of the local Persian authorities, Egyptian soldiers from Syene forced their way into the temple, plundered it, and burned it. Full of indignation and bitterness, the Jewish writers observe that their temple had stood for over a century, since before the time of Cambyses. They go on to describe the community's liturgical response: wearing of sackcloth, fasting, abstention from sexual relations, and a vindictive curse against the hated Persian governor, Vidranga, reminiscent in tone of the conclusion to Psalm 137. The writers allude to complaints, never answered, which they sent to religious officials in Jerusalem immediately after the event. They also state that reports were sent to Samaria, to the administrative authorities Delayah and Shelemyah, sons of Nehemiah's old nemesis, Sanballat (Sin-uballit). The administrative relationship between Judah and Samaria at this time remains one of the many historical unknowns of the period. Yedanyah and his associates take care to exonerate the satrap Arshama from any complicity in the outrage.

No. 35 is the reply — or rather a succinct memorandum giving the gist of the reply — perhaps taken down orally from a courier. The Judean governor Bagavahya and Delayah of Samaria grant permission for the temple to be reconstructed, and its meal and incense offerings restored. Notably absent is any permission to reinstitute animal sacrifice, as the petitioners had requested. Whether this is an accommodation to Egyptian sensitivities or a desire on the part of Persian and Jewish authorities in Palestine to downgrade the importance of the Elephantine shrine is unknown.

Letter No. 36 belongs to the same sequence of events, although its relationship to No. 35 is unclear. Like No. 35, it is a rough draft or an abbreviated file copy. The unnamed addressee was probably Arshama, the satrap (see the introduction to chapter 5), for his permission to rebuild would surely have been required. Conceding the restriction against animal sacrifice, the community leaders ask for permission to rebuild, offering a "donation" (evidently a euphemism for a bribe) to encourage the recipient to decide in their favor.

Whether the temple was actually rebuilt is impossible to say. Legal documents dated after 407 describe nearby property lines with reference to the temple precincts. But the site could have been used as a reference point even if it remained in ruins. If the sanctuary was restored, it was not used for long. The last datable document from the Jewish colonists is a fragmentary letter (not included here) from 399 B.C.E. alluding to the accession of the Egyptian king Nepherites, founder of the Twenty-ninth dynasty (Kraeling 1953: No. 13). With the end of Persian hegemony in Egypt, the colony vanished without a trace.

===== Passover (?) and Unleavened Bread =====

30a. AP 21 (Berlin, St. Mus. P. 13464)
(419 B.C.E.)

A

1   [אל אחי י]דניה וכנותה ח[ילא] יהודיא אחוכם חננ[י]ה שלם אחי
אלהיא [ישאלו]

2   [בכל עדן] וכעת שנתא זא שנת 5 דריוהוש מלכא מן מלכא שליח על
ארש[ם . . .]

3   ] . . . .[יא כעת אנתם כן מנו ארבע

[. . . .

4   [יומן לניסן . . . . עב]דו ומן יום 15 עד יום 21
ל[. . . . .]

5   ] . . . . [דכין הוו ואזדהרו
עבידה א[ל תעבדו]

6   ] . . . .[אל תשתו וכל מנדעם זי חמיר אל
[תאכלו]

B

7   ] . . . . ב]מערב שמשא עד יום 21
לניס[ן . . . . .]

8 [...........................] ה]נעלו בתוניכם וחתמו בין
יומיא] אלה[

9 [....].א[

10 [אל] אחי ידניה וכנותה חילא יהודיא אחוכם חנניה ב]ר [...

[To my brothers,] Yedanyah and his colleagues, the Jewish [garrison], from your brother Hananyah.

May the gods bless my brothers [always].

This year, year five of King Darius, the king sent to Arshama [. . .]. You should count as follows: four[. . .]. And from the fifteenth day to the twenty-first day of [. . .].

Be scrupulously pure. Do not [do] any work [. . .]. Do not drink any [. . .] nor [eat] anything leavened. [. . . at] sunset until the twenty-first day of Nisan [. . .]. Bring into your chambers [. . .] and seal [. . .] during [these] days. [. . .].

Address: [To] my brothers Yedanyah and his colleagues, the Jewish garrison, from your brother Hananyah son of [. . .].

30b. AP 21 (Restored Version)

A

1 [אל אחי י]דניה וכנותה ח]וילא[יהודיא אחוכם חננ]י[ה שלם אחי
אלהיא]ישאלו[

2 [בכל עדן] וכעת שנתא זא שנת 5 דריוהוש מלכא מן מלכא שליח על
ארש]ם לאמר[

3 [..............................].יא כעת אנתם כן מנו ארב]עת
עשר[

4 [ויומן לניסן וכ 14 בין שמשיא פסחא עב]דו ומן יום 15 עד יום 21
ל]ניסן חגא[

5 [זי פטיריא אבדו שבעת יומן פטירן אכלו כעת] דכין הוו ואזדהרו
עבידה א]ל תעבדו[

6 [ביום 15 וביום 23 לניסן כל שכר]אל תשתו וכל מנדעם זי חמיר אל
]תאכלו[

B

7 |ואל יתחזי בבתיכם מן יום 14 לניסן ב]מערב שמשא עד יום 21
    לניסן[ן במערב]

8   ]שמשא וכל חמיר זי איתי לכם בבתיכם ה]נעלו בתוניכם וחתמו בין
    יומיא[ן אלה]

9   [....]א

10]אל[אחי ידניה וכנותה חילא יהודיא אחוכם חנניה בר[. . .]

[To my brothers,] Yedanyah and his colleagues, the Jewish [garrison], from
your brother Hananyah.

May the gods bless my brothers [always].

This year, year five of King Darius, the king sent to Arshama [saying: . . .].
You should count as follows: four[*teen days of Nisan—on the fourteenth day at
twilight you shall cele*]brate [*the Passover*]. And from the fifteenth day to the
twenty-first day of [*Nisan, you shall celebrate the festival of Unleavened Bread. You
shall eat unleavened bread for seven days*].

Be scrupulously pure. Do not [do] any work [*on the fifteenth day and on the
21st day of Nisan*]. Do not drink any [*fermented drink*]. Do not [eat] anything
leavened, [*or let it be seen in your houses from the fourteenth day of Nisan at*] sunset
until the twenty-first day of Nisan [*at sunset . . .*]. Bring into your chambers
[*any leaven which you have in your houses*] and seal [it] up during [these] days.
[. . .].

Address: [To] my brothers Yedanyah and his colleagues, the Jewish garrison,
from your brother Hananyah son of [. . .].

================== **An Accusation and a Warning** ==================

31. AP 38 (Cairo P. 3435=J. 43472)
(Late fifth century B.C.E.)

A

1   אל מראי ידניה אוריה וכהניא זי יהו אלהא מתן בר ישביה ברכיה
    כר[ן . . . .]

2   עבדך מעוזיה שלם מראן[י אלה שמיא ישאל שגיא בכל עדן ו]לרחמן הוו
    קדם

3 אלה שמיא וכעת כזי וידרנג רב חילא מטא לאבוט אסרני על / דבר
אבן / צרף 1 זי

4 השכחו גניב ביד רכליא על אחרן צחא וחור עלימי עננו אשתדרו עם
וידרנג

5 וחרנופי בטלל אלה שמיא עד שזבוני כען הא אתין תמה עליכם אנתם
חזו עליהם

6 מה צבו ומלה זי צחא ‏חור‏ יבעה מנכם אנתם קמו קבלהם כן כזי מלה
באישה

7 לא יהשכחון לכם לכם ידיע זי חנום הו עלין מן זי חנניה במצרין
עד כען

8 ומה זי תעבדון לחור לב‏[א]ש‏כם עבדן [אנ]תם חור עלים חנניה אנתם
זולו מן בתין

B

9 נכסן לקבל זי ידכם מהשכחה הבו לה לא חסרן הו לכם בזך שלח אנה
עליכם הו

10 אמר לי שלח אגרת קדמתי [הן]לו חסרן שני‏א‏ שים אחדוהי בבית
עננו זי תעבדון

11 לה לא יתכסון מן עננו

12 אל מראי ידניה אוריה וכהניא ויהודיא ע‏[בד]כם מעותיה בר נתן

To my lords Yedanyah, Uriyah and the priests of the God YHW, Mattan son of Yeshobyah, Berekyah son of [. . . . from] your servant Mauzyah.

[May the God of heaven] bless my lords richly at all times, and may the God of heaven be merciful to you.

When commander Vidranga arrived in Abydos, he had me arrested on a charge relating to a stolen rhinestone(?) which was found in the hands of the merchants.[1] Anani's servants Seha and Hor stirred up such a commotion with Vidranga and Hornufi (with the help of God)[2] that they eventually got me released.

Now they are coming there to you. Watch out for them! What do they really want? Whatever Seha and Hor demand from you, stand up to them, so there won't be any unfortunate rumors against you. You are aware that Khnum[3] has been against us from the time Hananyah was in Egypt until now.

So if you help Hor, you are [hurting] yourselves. Hor is really Hananyah's man. Should you despise our own property? Give him just what he deserves;[4] it will not be your loss!

That is why I am writing to you. He said to me, "Send a letter ahead of me." If any serious loss is incurred, arrest him at Anani's house. Whatever you do to him will not be concealed from Anani.

Address: To my lords Yedanyah, Uriyah and the priests, and the Jews, from your servant Mauzyah son of Natan.

Riot and Imprisonment

32. AP 56+34
(Berlin, St. Mus. P. 13456=Cairo P. 3439=J. 43476)
(End of fifth century B.C.E.)

A

1 [אל אחי . . . אחוך יסלח שלם לי תנה]אלהיא ישאלו שלמך בכל עדן
וכעת [. . . . . .]

2 [. . . . .]י בר יׄחׄ[. .]אזל לסון ועבד
ליהוׄ[. . . . .]

3 [. . . . .] הא זנה שמהת גבריא ז]י אסירו ב[י]ב
ברכיא הוש[ע. . . . .]

4 [. . . . .] פחנום הא זנה שמהת
נשיא זי א[שתכחו בבבא]

5 [בנא ואתחדו א]סירן רמי אתת הודו אסרשות אתת הושע פלול אתת
יסלח רעיא [. . . . .]

6 תבלא ברת משלם קולא אחתה הא שמהת גבריא זי אשתכחו בבבא בנא
ואתחדו [אסירן]

7 ידניא בר גמריה הושע בר יתום הושע בר נתום חגי אחוהי אחיו
בר מכי[ה. . . . .]

8 בתיא זי עלו בהן ביב ונכסיא זי לקחו אתבו אם על מריהם להן
דכרו למרא[יהם כסף]

9 כרשן 120 עוד טעם לא עד יהוי להן תנה שלם ביתך ובניך עד
אלהיא יחוונ[ני אפיך בשלם]

B

10 [אל   אחי . . . . . בר] נדול אחן[ו]ך יסלח בר נתן

[To my brother . . . from your brother Yislah.
I am well here.] May the gods bless you always.
[. . .] son of [. . .] has gone to Syene and has made [. . .] for Yeho[. . .].
[These are the names of the men] who here imprisoned at Elephantine:
　　Berekyah
　　Hoshea
　　[*Several names are lost*]
　　Pakhnum.
These are the names of the women who were [found at the gate in Thebes
and taken] prisoner:[5]
　　Rami, wife of Hodaw
　　Isireshwet, wife of Hoshea
　　Pallul, wife of Yislah
　　Reiah [. . .]
　　Tabla, daughter of Meshullam
　　Qawwilah, her sister.
These are the names of the men who were found at the gate in Thebes and
were taken [prisoner]:
　　Yedanyah son of Gemaryah
　　Hoshea son of Yatom
　　Hoshea son of Nattum
　　Haggai, his brother
　　Ahyo son of Mikayah
[. . .] the houses they broke into at Elephantine and the goods they took.
I can confirm that they have returned them to their owners,[6] only they men-
tioned to the property-owners a sum of 120 silver *karsh*.[7] There is no need
for any further orders to be given here concerning them.
　　Greetings to your household and your children until the gods let me see
you again in good health!

Address: [To my brother . . . son of] Gaddul from your brother Yislah son of
Natan.

=== **Accusation of Stopping a Well** ===

33. AP 27 (U. of Strasbourg Library, P. Aram. 2)
(Ca. 410 B.C.E.)

A

1   לא מנטרתן אנחנה מרדו מצריא זי דגלן רבין אֹנֹחֹנֹה]תנגן[. . . .]
שבקן

2   כזי]מל[כא דרייהוש 14 מחבל לא אשתכח לן בשנת]{ומנדעם}[
מראן ארשם

3   ]עבד[ו ביב אזל על מלכא זנה דושכרתא זי כמריא זי חנוב אלהא
בירתא

4   המונית עם וידרנג זי פרתרך תנה הוה כסף ונכסן יהבו לה איתי קצת

5   מן יודנא זי מלכא זי ביב בירתא נדשו ושור חד בנין ב]מנציעת
בירת יב

6   וכען שורא זך בנה במנציעת בירתא איתי באר חדה זי בניה

7   בנ]נן בני[ן]רתא ומין לא חסרה להשקיא חילא כזי הן הנדיז יהוון

8   בברא]ז[ך מיא שתין כמריא זי חנוב אלך ברא זך סכרו הן אזד

9   יתעבד מן דיניא תיפתיא נושכיא זי ממנין במדינת תשטרם

10   יתי]דע[ן למראן לקבל זנה זי אנחנה אמרן אף פרישן אנחנה

B

11   ] . . . . [רֹחפניא זי ביב בן]ירתא . . . . [

12   ] . . . . [ ]ן אנחנה רבין] . . . . [

13   ] . . . . [ ]ה לא אשתכח ל]ן . . . . [

14   ] . . . . [ ]יא להיתיה מנ]חנה . . . . [

15   ] . . . . [למעבד תמה ליהו א]להא . . . . [

16   ] . . . . [ ]מ[. . .]בנו [.]לה [. . . . . . . [

17   ] . . . . [להן אתרודן חדה] . . . . [

18   ] . . . . [אשרנא לקחו לנפש]הום . . . . [

19   ] . . . . [ה]ן על מראן ֿט֞ב שגיא עש]ן . . . . [

20   ] . . . . [ ]ד אנחנה מן חילא] . . . . [

21 [. . .] הן על] מראן טב יתשים [טעם . . . .]

22 [. . . . .] אנחנה הן על מן]ראן טב [. . . . .]

23 [. . . . . .] יה]גנון למנדעעמתא זי או] [. . . . .]

24 [. . . .] אגור]א זי לן זי נדשו ל] [. . . . .]

[*Beginning missing*] We . . . . our officers. The Egyptian garrison troops rioted, but we did not abandon our posts and were not personally injured.[8]

In the year fourteen of King Darius when our lord Arshama returned to visit the court, this is the offense which the priests of Khnum committed in Fort Elephantine in collusion with Vidranga, the governor here. (They gave him a bribe of money and goods.)

There is a portion of the royal storehouse(?) in Fort Elephantine. They tore it down and built a wall in the middle of Fort Elephantine. The wall is still standing right in the middle of the fortress.

There was a well built inside the fortress, so that the garrison had no lack of drinking water. Whenever we were confined[9] inside the fortress, we could drink water from that well. Those priests of Khnum stopped up the well.

If a hearing on the matter of this report is held before the judges, police and investigators appointed over the district of Tshetres, the facts will become known to our lord. We are free of[10] [*any guilt in the matter*].

[. . .] of Fort Elephantine [. . .]. We [. . .] our officers [. . .] is not found [. . .] to bring a meal-offering [. . .] to do [. . .] there for [the God] YHW [. . .] inside [. . .] except a brazier(?) [. . .]. They took the fittings(?) for themselves [. . .].

If it please our lord, [. . .] greatly [. . .] we of the garrison [. . . If it] please our lord, let [an order] be issued [. . .]. We [. . .]. If it [please our lord . . .] they [pro]tect the things which [. . .] to [. . .] our [. . .], which they tore down.[11]

=== **Razing of Temple and Petition for Aid** ===

34. AP 30/31 (Berlin, St. Mus. P. 13495/ Cairo P. 3428=J. 43465) (November 25, 407 B.C.E.)

["Text A" (AP 30)]

A (Recto)

1 אל מראן בגוהי פחת יהוד עבדיך ידניה וכנותה כהניא זי ביב

בירתא שלם

2　מראן אלה שמיא ישאל שניא בכל עדן ולרחמן ישימנך קדם דריוהוש
מלכא

3　ובני ביתא יתיר מן זי כען ‏ªחד אלף‏ª וחין אריכן ינתן לך וחדה
ושריר הוי בכל עדן

4　כען עבדך ידניה וכנותה‏bl כן אמרן בירח תמוז שנת 14　דריוהוש מלכא
כזי ארשם

5　נפק ואזל על מלכא‏c כמריא זי חנוב ‎^אלהא^‎ זי ביב בירתא‏dהמונית עם
וידרנג זי פרתרך‏d תנה

6　הוה לם אגורא זי יהו אלהא זי ביב בירתא יהעדו מן תמה אחר‏e
וידרנג זך

7　לחיא אגרת שלח על נפין ברה זי רב ‎/‎ חיל הוה בסון בירתא לאמר
אגורא זי‏fi ביב

8　בירתא ינדשו אחר נפין‏g דבר מצריא עם חילא אחרנן אתו לבירת יב עם
תליהם‏h

9　עלו באגורא זך נדשוהי עד ארעא ועמודיא זי אבנא זי הוו תמה תברו
‎^המו^‎ אף הוה תרען

10　‏iזי אבן 5　בנין פסילה‏j זי אבן זי הוו באגורא זך נדשו ודשיהם
קימן וציריהם

11　זי דששיא אלך נחש ומטלל עקהן ‎^זי^‎ ארז כלא זי‏k עם שירית אשרנא
ואחרן זי תמה

12　הוה כלא באשה‏l שרפו ומזרקיא זי זהבא ‏mוכסף‏m ומנדעמתא זי הוה
באגורא זך כלא לקח‎^ו^‎

Textual notes on No. 34: variants in Text B (AP 31)

a The length of the lacuna in B suggests that these words were omitted.
b B seems to have been longer at this point.
c B seems to have been longer at this point.
d כסף ונכסין יהבו לוידרנג פרתרכא זי.
e Inserted above the line in B.
f B inserts יהו אלהא ביב.
g B inserts זך.
h זניהום.
i רברבן.
j פסלה.
k אגורא זך כלא עקהן זין] ארז.
l באשתא.
m B inserts וזי כספא.

13 ולנפשהום עבדו ומן יומיⁿ מלך מצרין אבהין בנו אנורא זך ביב
בירתא וכזי כנבוזי על למצר‸ין‸

14 אנורא זך בנה השכחה ואנורי אלהי מצרין כל° מגרו ואיש מנדעם
באנורא זך לא חבל

15 וכזי כזנה עביד אנחנה עם נשין ובנין שקקן לבשן הוין וצימין
ומצלין ליהו מרא שמיא

16 זי החויןᵖ בוידרנג זך כלᵇיא הנפקו כבלאᵠ מן רגלוהי וכל נכסין זי
קנה אבדו וכל ᵣגברין

17 זי בעוᵣ באיש לאנורא זך כלˢ קטילו וחזין בהום אף קדמת זנה בעדן
זי זא באיש‸תא‸

B (Verso)

18 עביד לן אגרה‸שלחן מראן ועלᵗ יהוחנן כהנא רבא וכנותה כהניא זי
בירושלם ועל אוסתן אחוה‸י‸

19 זי עננו וחרי יהודיאᵘ אגרה חדה לא שלחו עלין אף מן ירח תמוז שנת
14 דריהוש מלכא

20 וע‸ד‸ זנה יומא אנחנה שקקן לבשן וצימין נשיא זילן כארמלה
עבידין משח לא משחיןᵛ

21 וחמר לא שתין אף מן ᵂזכי ועד יוםᵂ שנת   17   דריהוש מלכא מנחה
ולבונ‸נ‸הˣ ועלוה

22 לא עבדו באנורא זך כען עבדיך ידניה וכנותהᵧ ויהודיאᵤ כלᶻ בעלי
יב כן אמרי‸ןᵃᵃ

ⁿ יום.
° [כ]ל‸א‸ (?).
ᵖ חוינא.
ᵠ כבלוהי.
ʳ [גבר זין] בעה.
ˢ כלא.
ᵗ על זנה [שלחן] שלחן על מראן [א]ף על.
ᵘ יהוד.
ᵛ משחן.
ᵂ זך ע[נ]ד[נ]א ועד זנה יומא].
ˣ B omits -ו.
ᵧ B appears to have an additional phrase in the lacuna.
ᶻ כלא.
ᵃᵃ אמרן.

23 הן על מראן טב אתעשת על אגורא זך למבנה בזי לא שבקן לן למבניה
חזי בעלי

24 טבתך ורחמיך ˆזיˆ תנה במצרין אגרה מנך ישתלח עליהום על אגורא
זי יהו אלהא

25 למבניה ביב בירתא לקבל זי בנה הוה קדמין ומחתאˣbb ולבונתא ועלותא
יןˣˣ}{ה}ˣˣ}ˣˣcc קרבון

26 על מדבחא זי יהו אלהא בשמך ונצלה עליך בכל עדן אנחנה ונשין
ובנין ויהודיא

27 כלˣdd זי תנה הן כןˣee יעבדו עד זיˣˣee אגורא זך יתבנה וצדקה יהוה לך
קדם יהו אלה

28 שמיא מן גבר זי יקרב לה עלוה ודבחןˣff דמן כדמי כסף כנכרין 1   לף
ועל זהב על זנה

29 שלחן הודען אף כלאˣff מליא באגרהˣgg חדה שלחןˣhh ˆבשמןˆ ˣhh על דליה
ושלמיה בני סנאבלט פˆחˆת שמרין

30 אף בזנהˣii ˆזי עביד לן ˆכלאˆˣii ארשם לא ידע ב   20   למרחשון שנת
17   דריהוש מלכא

To our lord Bagavahya, governor of Judah from your servants Yedanyah and his colleagues the priests at Fort Elephantine.

May the God of Heaven richly bless our lord always, and may he put you in the good graces of King Darius and his household a thousand times more than now. May he grant you long life, and may you always be happy and strong!

Your servant Yedanyah and his colleagues report to you as follows:

In the month of Tammuz in the fourteenth year of King Darius, when Arshama left and returned to visit the court, the priests of the god Khnum in Fort Elephantine, in collusion with Vidranga,[12] the military governor here, said, "Let us get rid of the temple of the god YHW in Fort Elephantine!"

---

bb *Sic!* The word is lost in B, but would presumably have been corrected to ומנחתא.
cc נקרב.
dd כלא.
ee תעבד זי עד.
ff {{בכלא}} [*lacuna*] דמי כסף כנכרן אלף על. The lacuna evidently contained a text slightly longer than that of A.
gg אגרה.
hh בשמן שלחן.
ii B adds כלא זי עביד לן.

Then that criminal Vidranga wrote a letter to his son Nafaina, commandant at Fort Syene, as follows, "Let the temple[13] in Elephantine be destroyed!"
So Nafaina came at the head of some Egyptian and other troops to Fort
Elephantine with their pickaxes.[14]

They forced their way into the temple and razed it to the ground, smashing
the stone pillars there. The temple had five[15] gateways built of hewn stone,
which they wrecked. They set everything else on fire: the standing doors and
their bronze pivots, the cedar roof—everything, even the rest of the fittings
and other things. The gold and silver basins and anything else they could find
in the temple, they appropriated for themselves!

Our ancestors built that temple in Fort Elephantine back during the time
of the kings of Egypt, and when Cambyses came into Egypt, he found it
already built. They pulled down the temples of the Egyptian gods, but no
one damaged anything in that temple.

After this had been done to us, we with our wives and our children put
on sackcloth, and fasted and prayed to YHW the lord of heaven:

> "Show us our revenge on that Vidranga:
> May the dogs tear his guts out from between his legs!
> May all the property he got perish!
> May all the men who plotted evil against that temple—
> all of them—be killed!
> And may we watch them!"

Some time ago, when this evil was done to us, we sent letters to our lord,
to Yehohanan the high priest and his colleagues the priests in Jerusalem, to
Avastana, brother of Anani, and to the Judean nobles. None of them ever replied
to us.

From the month of Tammuz in the fourteenth year of King Darius until
this very day, we have continued wearing sackcloth and fasting. Our wives
are made like widows. We do not anoint ourselves with oil, nor do we drink
wine. And from that time until this, the seventeenth year of King Darius, no
meal offering, incense or burnt offering has been offered in the temple.

Now your servants Yedanyah, his colleagues, and all the Jews, citizens of
Elephantine, petition you as follows:

If it please our lord, let consideration be given to the rebuilding of this temple,
for they are not allowing us to rebuild it. Take care of your loyal clients and
friends here in Egypt. Let a letter be sent to them from you concerning the
temple of the God YHW, allowing it to be rebuilt in Fort Elephantine just
as it was formerly. If you do so, meal offerings, incense and burnt offerings
will be offered in your name on the altar of the God YHW. We will pray for
you constantly—we, our wives, our children, the Jews—everyone here.

If they do this until the temple is rebuilt,[16] it will be a righteous deed on
your part before the God YHW, more so than if one were to offer him burnt
offerings and sacrifices worth a thousand silver talents, and gold.

Thus we have written to inform you. We also reported the entire matter in a letter in our name to Delayah and Shelemyah, sons of Sin–uballit (Sanballat), governor of Samaria. Also, Arshama did not know anything about all these things that were done to us.

Date: The twentieth of Marheshwan, seventeenth year of King Darius

=========== **Memorandum on Reconstructing the Temple** ===========

35. AP 32 (Berlin, St. Mus. P. 13497)
(Shortly after 407 B.C.E.)

1 זכרן זי בנוהי ודליה אמרו
2 לי זכרן לם יהוי לך במצרין לממר ‏{{קד}}
3 קדם ארשם על בית מדבחא זי אלה ‏{{שמי}}
4 שמיא זי ביב בירתא בנה
5 הוה מן קדמן קדם כנבוזי
6 זי וידרנג לחיא זך נדש
7 בשנת 14 דריוהוש מלכא
8 למבניה באתרה כזי הוה לקדמן
9 ומנחתא ולבונתא יקרבון על
10 מדבחא זך לקבל זי לקדמין
11 הוה מתעבד

Memorandum: What Bagavahya and Delayah said to me:
  Let this be on record for you in Egypt.

Official of Record: Arshama.

Concerning: The temple of the God of Heaven which was built at Fort Elephantine long ago, before the time of Cambyses, which "that criminal Vidranga" razed in the fourteenth year of King Darius.

Let it be rebuilt on its original site and let meal offerings and incense be offered up on the altar just as was formerly done.

A Petition and a Bribe

36. AP 33 (Cairo P. 3430=J. 43467)
(Shortly after 407 B.C.E.)

1 עבדיך ידניה בר גמ[ריה] שמה 1

2 מעוזי בר נתן שמה [1]

3 שמעיה בר חגי שמה 1

4 הושע בר יתום שמה 1

5 הושע בר נתון שמה 1 כל גברין 5

6 סונכנן זי ביב בירתא מה[חס]נן

7 כן אמרן הן מראן [. . .]

8 ואגורא זי יהו אלהא זילן יתבנה

9 ביב בירתא כזי קדמן ב[נ]ה הוה

10 וקן תור ענז מקלו [ל]א יתעבד תמה

11 להן לבונה מנחה [. . . . .]

12 ומראן אודים יעב[ד . . . .]

13 נתן על בית מראן כ[ן . . . . . .]

14 שערן ארדבן אל[ף]

Your servants named below:
> Yedanyah son of Gemaryah
> Mauzi son of Natan
> Shemayah son of Haggai
> Hoshea son of Yatom
> Hoshea son of Nattun

—five men in all (Syenians, who hold property in Fort Elephantine)—
We declare as follows:

If our lord [*will give permission*] for the temple of our God YHW to be rebuilt in Fort Elephantine as it was previously, we agree that no sheep, ox or goat is to be offered as a burnt offering, but only incense and meal offering.

[If] our lord will make a ruling [on the matter], we will make a donation to our lord's household of [. . . of silver], and 1000 *ardabs* of barley.

Notes

1. The word *rkly'* means either "merchants" (perhaps referring to receivers of stolen goods) or "slanderers" (i.e., false witnesses). In either case, Mauzyah implies that the charges against him were false.

2. Literally, "in the shadow of the God of heaven." The sense may be "under oath" or "under safe conduct."

3. Apparently a faction associated with the Egyptian temple of Khnum at Elephantine is meant.

4. Literally, "Whatever your hand finds, give it to him"; cf. 1 Sam 10:7.

5. The word "gate" may refer to a law court. If so, we may translate, ". . . who were tried at the court in Thebes, and were put in prison."

6. Or, following Porten and Yardeni (1986: 60), "[They left] the houses they had broken into at Yeb, and did indeed return to their owners the goods they had taken."

7. The vaguely worded sentence may refer to a penalty negotiated between the householders and the defendants, or it may hint obliquely at a bribe. One hundred twenty *karsh* was an immense sum, some ten kilograms (twenty-two pounds) of silver, equivalent to nearly eight year's income for a small family (Porten 1968: 75).

8. Or "We were not found to be at fault."

9. Or "mobilized."

10. Or "we are separated from [. . .]."

11. Porten and Yardeni (1986: 64) restore, ". . . to [*build*] our [*Temp*]le which they demolished." However, it is not clear that the text refers to the events described in No. 34.

12. For this phrase, B. reads, ". . . offered a bribe of silver and goods to Vidranga."

13. B adds: "of the God YHW."

14. B: "weapons."

15. B adds: "great."

16. B: "If you act so that the temple may be rebuilt. . . ."

V

Letters from Persian Officials

Introduction

All but one of the letters in this chapter were acquired by the Bodleian Library at Oxford in 1943–44, and published by G. R. Driver in 1954. No details concerning their discovery are known, but it is clear from internal evidence that they were found in Egypt, possibly at Memphis or somewhere in the western Delta. They were written on leather and were found stored in a leather bag that contained between fifteen and twenty documents, some of which are now too fragmentary to be read. Twelve are included here (Nos. 37–48).

All twelve letters are associated with Arshama, satrap of Egypt during the last half of the fifth century. Most are from him, and the rest concern officials closely associated with him. Since the letters are undated, their sequence cannot be determined, except for the general observation that Nos. 37–40 are earlier than Nos. 41–48. In the latter group, Nakhthor holds the position that earlier belonged to Psamshek ("the former steward," No. 43). A thirteenth letter from Arshama's administration, written on papyrus (No. 49), was found at Elephantine. All of these letters deal with administrative concerns.

Most, perhaps all, of the letters in the group of twelve originated outside of Egypt. They were not all written from the same place. Nos. 44 and 45, taken together, place Arshama in Babylon. Yet No. 47 implies that he is *not* in Babylon, since he has to communicate with an associate there by letter. Susa, the primary seat of the Persian government, is a likely alternative (cf. Nos. 33 and 46).

The letters cover several years. Driver suggests that they were sent during Arshama's prolonged absence from Egypt in 410–407, referred to in the letters of chapter 4 (Nos. 33 and 34), but that is most uncertain. There must have been other such trips to transport rents, goods, and slaves and to deal with other details of administering Arshama's lands

71

72 Letters from Persian Officials

in Mesopotamia and Syria. The letters in this chapter and those in chapter 4 both speak of insurrections. Such events happened repeatedly throughout the fifth century, however, and without more information we are often unable to correlate them for dating purposes. No. 49, the one dated letter in the chapter, was written in 411 B.C.E. Nothing in it implies that Arshama was away from Egypt at the time.

A good deal is known about Arshama from Greek and ancient Near Eastern sources. Achaemenes, his predecessor as satrap of Egypt, was a brother of King Xerxes, and Arshama himself was a kinsman of the royal family. Although the Aramaic texts refer to him as "Prince Arshama," his exact relationship to the king is unknown. Appointed by Artaxerxes I in 454, in the aftermath of the rebellion of Inaros (see the introduction to chapter 2), he held office for half a century, passing from the scene just before Egypt rebelled anew at the end of the fifth century.

In the letters relating to the destruction of the Elephantine temple (chapter 4), the writers state repeatedly that Arshama was away from Egypt and had no involvement in the incident. He apparently took an extended leave in Babylonia and Persia between 410 and 407. Arshama was an exceedingly wealthy absentee master of a network of estates scattered throughout the empire. The letters in this chapter refer to his estates in Upper and Lower Egypt; cuneiform texts preserve the financial records of grazing lands belonging to him in central Babylonia; and letter No. 41 alludes to additional domains in Assyria and Syria.

Other names keep recurring in the letters. There is Psamshek the steward, Egyptian overseer of Arshama's estates, apparently in both Upper and Lower Egypt (Nos. 37–39; cf. No. 43 for the restoration of the title in No. 37). We meet him later in charge of a slave convoy in Babylon (No. 47). There is Nakhthor, the Egyptian who took over Psamshek's job as steward, performing so incompetently that he found himself forced to answer charges of mismanagement (No. 43), theft, and personal abuse of the household staff (No. 47). There is the Persian Artavant (Nos. 37, 39–40), never addressed by a title, but apparently Arshama's second in command. There is Prince Varuvahya, a Persian absentee landlord residing in Babylon and a peer of Arshama (Nos. 44–45).

Except for No. 49, the letters deal with estate management, concerns such as the appointment of stewards (Nos. 37 and 42), payment of rents (44, 45), and administrative complaints of various sorts. Two letters concern slaves. No. 39 authorizes punishment of a number of slaves who escaped from a transport convoy, and No. 40 demands the release of a group of slaves wrongly imprisoned during an uprising. Another (No. 38) threatens to discipline an officer who will not obey the orders of Arshama's chief steward. Estate managers had no formal authority in military matters, so far as we know, but local commanders were expected to look after the interests of the satrap.

Three letters call for more extended comment. No. 41 is a requisition for rations for a traveling party headed by Nakhthor that was bound for Egypt. Although sometimes described as a "passport," it is neither that nor an official authorization for travel rations—though such documents have been found at Persepolis (Hallock 1985: 588–91). The letter is issued on Arshama's personal authority, addressed to six of his estate managers in Mesopotamia and Syria, and authorizes supplies only while the group is passing through his domains. Vast areas outside his jurisdiction are not covered. Of course, the distinction between "official" and "personal" authority would have been blurred in the case of such a highly placed personage. The group was authorized to sojourn only one day at each place (cf. *Did.* 11:5).

For the first part of its journey the party appears to have followed the famous "Royal Road" described by Herodotus (*History* 5.52–53). This well-engineered and well-guarded highway, equipped with royal staging posts and caravansaries, ran from Susa northward and westward across the empire all the way to Sardis, some 2,500 km. (1,600 mi.) distant, with a connecting link to Ephesus on the Mediterranean coast. Royal mounted couriers were said to traverse it in a week; a party on foot required three months.

Nakhthor's group, perhaps starting out in Susa, would have followed this road northwest through Arrapha (modern Kirkuk). Lairu (biblical Lair, 2 Kgs 19:13) lay somewhere along the first part of the route, in northeastern Babylonia near the Elamite border. From Arrapha they would have proceeded northwest to Arbela, ancient cult city of the Assyrian goddess Ishtar, where Arshama had another estate. The Arzuhina estate was apparently in the same general region, as were possibly some of the other sites mentioned in the letter (Driver 1965: 56–59; Cogan and Tadmor 1988: 235). Following the highway northwest of Arbela, the party would have crossed the Tigris at Nineveh (near Mosul).

At that point they would have left the Royal Road. An ancient Assyrian road running westward past Guzanu (Tell Halaf) and Haran would offer a more direct route. Near Haran they could have turned south, following a secondary road down to the Euphrates highway. Then, if there existed a desert shortcut to Tadmor (Palmyra), that would have been the quickest way to Damascus. Otherwise, they would have taken the longer road through Aleppo and Hamath (Hama). From Damascus, the route is straightforward: south through Hazor and Megiddo to the coast road down to Egypt (see the map).

A second unusual letter (No. 46) contains a unique commission to one of Arshama's artisans in Egypt to prepare several sculptures or statuettes for him: two were on an equestrian theme, the others not specified. The fact that the sculptor was known in Susa suggests that he was an artist of some repute among the Persian aristocracy.

Persian ruling circles had great admiration for the skill of Egyptian artisans. A century before this letter was written, Darius I (522–486) used Egyptian goldsmith, wood-workers, and other artisans in the construction of his new palace at Susa, and Egyptian themes are widely found in Persian art. Among the Achaemenid artistic creations that can still be seen are a stylized gold statuette of a horseman (Dandamaev and Lukonin 1989: 272) and another of a chariot with a driver, a soldier, and a three-horse team. The front of the chariot depicts the Egyptian god Bes (Gershevitch 1985: pl. 44a). Egyptian motifs also appear on Persian seals (Gershevitch 1985: pl. 48ab).

The third text for special comment is No. 49, the only administrative document found at Elephantine that relates to Arshama. It concerns repairs to a boat. The most difficult letter in this collection, it is full of untranslatable shipyard jargon and technical terms, some of which are loanwords from Egyptian and Persian, and some of which are quite unknown.

The chancery scribes' habit of giving an epitome of earlier correspondence allows us to see in this letter the operation of the Achaemenid bureaucracy at its most convoluted. Four levels of previous administrative action are summarized before getting down to the business at hand (see Whitehead 1974: 124).

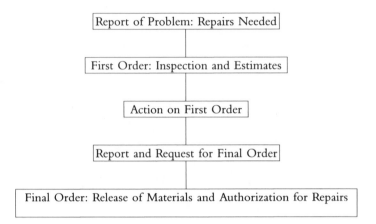

Report of Problem: Repairs Needed

First Order: Inspection and Estimates

Action on First Order

Report and Request for Final Order

Final Order: Release of Materials and Authorization for Repairs

The letter is signed by "Anani the scribe, Chancellor." His identity is unknown. He has been described as a Jew who rose to the position of chancellor at Arshama's headquarters in Memphis. However, several "Anani's" are known among the Jews at Elephantine, and the name is not distinctively Jewish (Stark 1971: 106; Benz 1972: 382). The letter does not specify where he is, and it is not known whether the title "chancellor" was used in more than one level of government. His office could have been at Memphis or in the regional chancery at Syene. There are no clear grounds for identifying him with the Anani mentioned in No. 31.

On arrival, these letters passed through the hands of Egyptian file clerks who left their mark. One added his name in Demotic on the outside of Nos. 44 and 46, and the notations on No. 49 include a longer note in Demotic.

══════ Appointment of a Steward ══════

37. AD 2 (Bodleian Pell. Aram. XII)
(Provenance Unknown, Written from Babylon or Susa;
late fifth century B.C.E.)

A

1 מן ארשם על אר[תונ]ת שלם ושררת שֹגֹיֹ[ין]אֹ הושרת לֹךְ וכעת דשנא
מן מֹ[ן]לכא ומני יהב לעחחפי

2 עלימא זילי זי פק[ניד] הֹוֹה בין בניא זילי זי בנֹ[עֹ]ליתא . . . . . .
פסמֹ[ן]שֹךְ ברה זי עחחפי זי כען

3 פֹ[ן]קֹ[ני]ד עבד חלפוהי בין בניא זילי זי בעליתא [. . . . .]
דֹ[שֹ]נא זכי זֹ[יֹ]ןֹ מן מלכא ומני

4 י]הב לעחחפי פסמשך ברה שליט יהוי למנשא דשנא זכי תמה במ]צ[רין

B

5 מ]ן ארשם ברביתן]א[על]ארתונת . . . . [
6 על דשנא
7 זי עֹחֹחֹפֹי
8 פֹּקֹידֹא זֹי
9 [. . . . .]

From Arshama to [Artavant]
I send you greetings and best wishes for your good health.

Concerning: The [grant] given by the king and by me to my man Ahhapi,
who has been steward of my various estates in [Upper and Lower Egypt].

Ahhapi's son Psamshek, who has now been given his father's position as
steward of my various estates in Upper [and Lower Egypt, has requested] that
the grant given by the king and by me be transferred to him.
Psamshek is hereby authorized to receive said grant there in Egypt.

Address: From Prince Arshama to [Artavant in Egypt].
Docket: Concerning the grant of Ahhapi the steward who [. . .].

========= **Reprimand to an Insubordinate Officer** =========

38. AD 4 (Bodleian Pell. Aram. II)
(Provenance Unknown, Written from Babylon or Susa;
late fifth century B.C.E.)

A

1 מן ארשם על ארמפי וכעת פסמשך / פקידא זילי שלח עלי כן אמר ארמפי
עם חילא זי לידה לא משתמען לי

2 בצבות מראי זי אמר אנֹה להם כעת ארשם כן אמֹ]ר[צבות ביתא זילי זי
פסמשך יאמר לך ולחילא זי לידך זכי

אשתמעו לה ועבדו כן ינׁדׁיעׁ יׁ]הוה לך הן פסמשׁ[ך אׁ]חר קבלת מנך   3

ישלח עלי חסן תשתאל ונסת פתגם

יתעבד לך בנסרו ידע טעׁמא זנה אחפפי ספרא   4

B

מן]אׁ[רׁשׁם על ארמפי   5

על זי פסמש]ך[6

אמר לא משתמ]ען[7

לי   8

From Arshama to Armapiya.
My steward Psamshek has informed me as follows:

> Armapiya and the troops under his command are refusing to obey the orders
> I have given them concerning my lord's affairs.

Now I, Arshama, declare:

In any matter concerning my household about which Psamshek gives orders
to you or the troops under your command, you are to obey those orders to
the letter! You have been warned. If Psamshek sends me another complaint
about you, you will be called strictly to account and will be severely disciplined.

Bagasrava has been informed of this order.

Ahpepi
Scribe

Address: From Arshama to Armapiya
Docket: Concerning Psamshek's report of insubordination.

===== **Slaves** =====

39. AD 3 (Bodleian Pell. Aram. VII+Frag. 7.1)
(Provenance Unknown, Written from Babylon or Susa;
late fifth century B.C.E.)

A

1   מן ארשם על ארתונת שלם ושררת שגיא הושרת לך ו]נכעת פס]מֹשך שמה בר
עחחפ]ין] עלימא זילי קבל

2   בזנה כן אמר כזי אנה הוֹיֹת אתהֹ]עֹ]ל]מֹרֹאֹי ..... עב]רֹן זי עחחפי
אבי זֹי אנה מן]......................

3   אחרי על מראי פסמשכחסי שמה]בר ....1 ..... בר....]טוי 1 עחחפי
בר פן]......1....[

4   בר פסמשך 1 פשובסתי בר חורן]1... בר ...1 .... [בר וחפרעמחי 1
[1 ...בר....]

5   כל גברן 8 נכסי לקחו וקרקו מני כען הן על מראי טב ישתלח על
ארתונֹתן כזי עבדיא כלך זין]

6   אהקרב קֹדמיהי סרושיתא זי אנה אשים / להם טעם יתעבד / להם כעת
ארשמן כן אמֹר פס]מן]שֹכחסי]

7   זכי וכנותה עבדי עחחפי זי]פֹס]מֹשך יהקרב קדמיך]תֹמה] אנת שם טעם
סרושן]ית]אֹ זי פסמשך]ישים]

8   להם טעם למעבד זכי יתעבד / להם

B

9   מן ארשם בר /]בֹיתא על ארתונת זי במצֹ]רין

From Arshama to Artavant:
I send you greetings and best wishes for your good health.
My man Psamshek son of Ahhapi has registered a complaint here as follows:

> While I was on the way to see my lord [. . .] slaves of my father Ahhapi,
> whom I [. . .] after me to my lord—
>   1. Psamshekhasi son of [. . .]
>   2. [. . .] son of [. . .]

3. Ahhapi son of [...]
4. [...] son of Psamshek
5. Pashubasti son of Hor
6. [...] son of [...]
7. [...] son of Wahpremahi
8. [...] son of [...].
(eight persons in all)
—took my property and ran away from me.

Now, if it please my lord, let word be sent to Artavant [that the slaves] I am
sending him should be punished as I have ordered.

Now I, Arshama, declare:
  In the matter of this Psamshekhasi and his companions, slaves of Ahhapi
whom Psamshek is sending to you there— you are to give orders that the
punishment demanded by Psamshek should be carried out.

Address: From [Prince] Arshama [to Artavant] in Egypt.

40. AD 5 (Bodleian Pell. Aram. IV)
(Provenance Unknown, Written from Babylon or Susa;
late fifth century B.C.E.)

A

1 מן ארשם על אׄרתהנת שלם ושררת שׁניא הושרת]לׄך[וכעת בזנה קדמי
שלם

2 אף תמה קדמ]יׄךׄ[שֵלם יהוי וכעת איתי גברן חיל]כין[עבדן זילי
במצרין

3 פרין]מׄ[אׄ שמה 1 אמון שמה 1 סרך שמה 1 תענדי]שׄ[מׄהׄ]1 . . . .[מׄיׄ שמה
1 סרסבנז שׄ]מׄ[הׄ]1[

4 אׄ]. .[ם שמה 1 סרמנז שמה 1 כא שמה 1 בנפרן שמה 1 פיתרענז שמה 1
אסמרוף

5 שמה 1 מוסרם שמה 1 כל גברן 13 אבשוכן ממנין הׄוׄוׄ בין בניא זילי
זי

6 בׄעליתא ותחתיתא אחר כזי מצרין מרדת וחילאׄ הנדיז הוו אדין

7 פרׄיׄמא זך וכנותה לא שנציו למנעל / בכירתא אחר] . .[נן .]רן לחיא
אחר המו

8 עמה הוו כען הן עליך כות טב מנך יתשם טעם כזי איש מנדעם באיש לא

9 יעבד לפירמא זך וכנותה ישתבקו עבידתא זילי יעבדו כזי קדמן

B

10 מן [א]רשם בר / ביתא על ארתהנת זי ב[נמצרי]ן
11 על חילכיא
12 [. . . .]זִיֹלֹיֹ
13 [.]שֹ[נ]ציו
14 [. .] למהוה

From Arshama to Artahant.[1]
I send you greetings and best wishes for your good health.
All is well with me here, may it also be well with you there.
There are certain Cilician slaves of mine in Egypt whose names are listed as follows:
1. Pariyama
2. Ammuwana
3. Saraka
4. [. . .]
5. [. . .]miya
6. Sadasbinazi
7. [. . .]
8. Sarmanazi
9. Ka
10. Bagafarna
11. Piyatarunazi
12. Asmaraupa
13. Muwasarma
(thirteen persons in all, pressers[?] who were appointed in my various estates in Upper and Lower Egypt).

When the Egyptians rebelled and the garrison had to be mobilized, this Pariyama and his co-workers were unable to get into the fortress. Later, that criminal [. . .] arrested them and has kept them in custody.

Now, if you concur, let an order be issued that no one is to harm Pariyama and his co-workers. They should be released and go back to work for me.

Address: From Prince Arshama to Artahant in [Egypt].
Docket: Concerning the Cilicians [. . .] my [. . .] were unable [. . .] to be [. . .].

===== **Rations for a Traveling Party** =====

41. AD 6 (Bodleian Pell. Aram. VII)
(Provenance Unknown, Written from Babylon or Susa; late fifth century B.C.E.)

1　מן ארשם על מרדך פקיד ה]א זי בן]א.]כד נבודל נ]ן֗ פקן י]דא[זי

בלער זתוהי פקידא [זי בא]ן[רוזחן אפסתבר פן]קי֗דא[זי בארבל

]חֹל֗ . [ומתלבש בנפרן֗ פֹקידא

2　[ז]י בסעלם פרדפרן והון . .]ת [פ]קין]די[א זי בדמשק [וכע]ת [וה]א֗

נחתחור שמה פקידא זינ]ל֗י אזן]ל֗י מצרין אנתנֹם[הבֹו [לה פן]תף

מן ביתא זילי זי במדינ֗תכם

3　יום ליום קמח חורי חפנן תרתן]ן קמח רמי חפנן תלת חמר או שכר

חפנן תרתין [. . .]ר חד ולעלימוהי גֹבֹן֗ר]ן[עשרה לחד ליומא

4　קמח חפן חדה עמיר֗ לקבל רכשה והבו פתף לנברן חלכין תרין אמן חד

כל תלתה עלימן זילי זי אזלן עמה מצרין לנבר

5　לנבר ליומא קמח חפן חדה פתפא זנה הבו להם מן פקיד על פקיד לקבל

אדונא זי מן מדינה עד מדינה עד ימטא מצרין

6　והן יהוה באתר חד יתיר מן יום חד אחר זי יומיא אלך יתיר פתף אל

תנתנו להם בנסרו ידע טעמא זנה רשת ספרֹא֗

From Arshama to:
　Marduk, official in [. . .]
　Nabu-delani, official in Lairu,
　Zatuvahya, official in Arzuhina,
　Upastabara, official in Arbela, [. . .] and Lubash
　Bagafarna, official in Saalam,
　Fradafarna and [. . .], officials in Damascus:

This is to introduce my official, Nakhthor by name. He is on his way to Egypt. You are to issue him daily provisions from my estates in your respective provinces as follows:

　White flour: 2 cups
　Fine[2] flour: 3 cups
　Wine or beer: 2 cups
　[. . .]: 1

For his retinue (ten men in all), for each one daily: Flour: one cup, plus sufficient fodder for his horses.

You are also to issue provisions to two Cilicians and one artisan (three in all), my servants, who are accompanying him to Egypt: Flour: one cup daily per man.

Issue these provisions, each official in turn, along the route from province to province, until he arrives in Egypt. If he stops in any place more than one day, do not give them any extra provisions for the additional days.

Bagasrava has been informed of this order.

Rashta
Scribe

Restoration of an Estate to Its Rightful Heir

42. AD 8 (Bodleian Pell. Aram. XIII)
(Provenance Unknown, Written from Babylon or Susa; late fifth century B.C.E.)

A

1   מן ארשם על נחתחור כנזסרם וכנותה וכעת פטוסרי שמה ורשבר עלים
[זי]לי שלח עלי כן אמר איתי פמון ש[נ]מֹה אבי כזי]

2   יוזא במצרין הוה זך אבד ובנה זי הוֹה מהחסן פמון שמה אבי בית זרע
א' 30   [זך אֹ]שתבק בנו בזי נשי ביתן כלא [אֹבדו . . . .]

3   לי בנה זי פמון אבי יתעשת / לי ינתנו / לי אהחסן כעת ארש[ם] כן /
אמר הן כֹנֹ[נֹ]ם הו כמליא אלה זי פטסרי שלח [עלי זי פמון]

4   [שֹ]מה אבוהי זך כזי יוזא הוה במצרין אבד עם נשי [ניתה ובֹנֹ]הֹ זי
פמוֹן זֹ]ך אֹבֹוֹהי בית זרע א' 30 זך אשתבֹ]ק [. . . . .]

5   לא עביד לעלים אחרן זילי מני לא יהיב אחר אנה בנה זי פמון זך
יהבת לפטסורי אנתם החווהי יהחסֹן והלכא

6   לקבל זי קדמן פמון אבוהי הוה חשל יחשל על ביתא זילי ארתוהי ידע
טעמא זנה רשת ספרא

B

7   מן ארשם על נחתחור פקידֹא [כנזֹס]רם וכנותה [המרכ]ריא זי
במצרין

From Arshama to Nakhthor, Kenzasirma, and his associates.

One of my tenant farmers,[3] Petosiri by name, has sent me word as follows:

> Concerning my father Pamun—he perished [during] the uprising in Egypt.
>
> The estate my father Pamun held a thirty-*ardab* plantation, was abandoned at that time, because all our household staff perished. The estate of my father Pamun [was not given] to me.
>
> I appeal to you. Let it be given to me to hold.

Now I, Arshama, declare:

If Petosiri has reported to [me] accurately,
- —that this Pamun, his father, perished along with [his household] staff,
- —that the estate of that Pamun, his father, a thirty-*ardab* plantation, was abandon[ed, . . . and]
- —that it was not made over [to my own estate,] or given by me to any other servant of mine,

then I give the estate of said Pamun to Petosiri.

You are to notify him. He will hold it and will pay the land-tax to my estate just as his father Pamun did formerly.

Artavahya has been informed of this order.

Rashta

Scribe

Address: From Arshama to Nakhthor the steward, Kenzasirma, and his associates the accountants in Egypt.

═══ Reprimand to a Negligent Steward ═══

43. AD 7 (Bodleian Pell. Aram. I)
(Provenance Unknown, Written from Babylon or Susa; late fifth century B.C.E.)

A

1   מן ארשׁם עַל נחתחור וכעת קדמן כֹּזי מצריא מרדו אדין ‹פ› סמשך פקידא

קדמיא גרדא ונכסיא /

2   זילנא [זין] בֹּמצרין חסין נטר כן כזי מנדעם כסנתו לא הוה מן ביתא

זילי אף מן אתר אחרן גרד

3 אמנן וסמ֫פֿזן ונכנ֫סן א֫נ֯חרנן שפיק בעה ועבד על ביתא זילי וכען תנה
כן שמיע לי כזי פקידיא זי

4 [בתח]תֹ֫יתא בשוזיא מתנצחן גרדֿא ונכֹ֫נֹסֹין מרנֿאֿינ֯הם חסֹ֫ין נטרן אף
אחרֿנ֯ן בעֹ֫ין מֹן אתֿר אחרן

5 ומהומֹ֫ספֿן עזֿל בית מראיהם ואנתם]כֹ[ן לא עבדן כען אף קדמן שלחת
עליכם על / זנֿ֫נ֯ה אנתם]אֿן֯[תֿנֹצחו / גרֿדא

6 ונכנֹ֫סֹיא זילֿי֯ן חסין טרו כן כזי מֹ֫נֹ֯נֹדֿ[עם כסנתו לא יהוה]מֹ[ן ביתא
זילי אף / מן אתר אֿן חֿ֯רן גרד אמנן

7 [וֹ]סספֿזן שֹ֫פיק בעו והנעלו בתרבצֿא זילי וסטרו בשנתא זילי ועבדו על
ביתא זֹ֫ילֹ֫י כן כזי פקידיא

8 [קדֿ]מֹ֫יא הוו עבדן כן ידיע יהוי לך הן / מן / גרדא או / מן נכסיא
אחרנן זילי מנדעם כסנתו יהוה

9 ומן אֿתֿֿר אחרן לא תבעון ולא תהוספֿון על / ביתא זילי / חסין
תשתאלון ונסת פתגם יתעבד

10 לֿך]אֿרן֯[תחי ידע טעמא זנה רשת ספרא

B

11 מֹן ארשם על נחתֿחֹ֫ור פקידֿא֫ זי במצרין בתחֿתיתא

12]עֹל[הֹ֯נדר]זֿא[

13 זֹי [. . . . .]

From Arshama to Nakhthor:

During the recent Egyptian uprising, Psamshek, the former steward went to great pains to guard our domestic staff and property in Egypt, so that my estate suffered no loss whatever. He even sought out additional staff, artisans of all kinds and property, and appropriated them for my estate.

Word has reached me here that the other stewards of Lower Egypt have been active during the recent outbreaks, going to great pains to guard their masters' personnel and property, seeking out others from elsewhere, and adding them to their masters' households. But you[4] have not been doing this.

I have written to you about this before. You are to care diligently for my staff and property so that my estate shall suffer no loss whatever. And you are to seek out additional staff, artisans of all kinds, and attach them to my service. Mark them with my mark, and put them to work in my estate, just as your predecessors used to do.

Know this: if any loss whatever to my staff or other property is incurred and you do not seek out replacements and add them to my household, you will be held strictly accountable, and will be severely punished.

Artahaya has been informed of this order.

Rashta,
Scribe

Address: From Arshama to Nakhthor, steward in Lower Egypt.
Docket: Concerning the instructions which [. . .].

=== **Overdue Rent** ===

44. AD 10 (Bodleian Pell. Aram. IX)
(Provenance Unknown, Written from Babylon or Susa;
late fifth century B.C.E.)

A

1 מן ארשם / על נחתחור כנזסרם וכנותה וכעת ורוהי בר ביתא בזנה כן
אמר לי בנא לם זי מן מראי יהיב / לי

2 במצרין זך מנדעם מן תמה לא מהיתין עלי הן על מראי לם כות טב
אגרת מן מראי תשתלח על נחתחור פקידא

3 והמרכריא כזי הנדרז יעבדון לחתובסמתי שמה פקידא זילי זי עד מנדת
בניא אלך יהנפק ויהיתה עלי עם מנדתא זי

4 מהיתה נחתנ]ה[ור כעת ארשם כן אמר אנתם הנדרז עבדו לחתובסתי פקיד
ורוהי זי עד מנדת בניא זי ורוהי אספרן

5 והדאבנו יהנפק ויהיתה ויאתה אם גנזא זי מני שים להיתיה בבאל
ארתוהי ידע טעמא זנה רשת ספרא

B

6 מן ארשם על נחתחור פקידא [כנז]סרם וכנותה המרכרן[י]א זי במצרין
7 על הנדרזא
8 זי [. . . . . . .]
9 [. . . . . . .]

[. . . . . . .]   10

⟨Demotic⟩   11

From Arshama to Nakhthor, Kenzasirma and his associates.
Prince Varuvahya has reported to me as follows:

Concerning: The estate given to me by my lord in Egypt.

Nothing has been brought to me from there. If it please my lord, let a letter
be sent to Nakhthor the steward and the accountants to the effect that they
should instruct my steward Hatubasti to release the rent for those estates
and send it to me along with the rent which Nakhthor is bringing.

Now I, Arshama, declare:

You are to instruct Hatubasti, Varuvahya's steward, to release the rent of
Varuvahya's estates — full payment with interest — and to bring it when you
come, along with the revenues I ordered brought to Babylon.

Artavahya has been informed of this order.

Rashta
Scribe

Address: From Arshama to Nakhthor the steward, Kenzasirma, and his associates
the accountants.
Docket: Concerning the instruction which [. . .].
Demotic notation: Hotephep.

45. AD 11 (Bodleian Pell. Aram. V)
(Provenance Unknown, Written from Babylon;
late fifth century B.C.E.)

A

1   מן ורוהי על נחתחור וכנדסירם וכנותה וכען֯ת֯ן] תנה אנה קבלת לארשם
על א֯ח֯תבסתי

2   פקידא זילי זי מ֯ן֯נדת֯א֯ן] מנדעם לא מהיתה לי אח֯ן֯ר . . . . .]ת מהית֯י֯ן
ן֯בבאל כ֯ע֯ן֯ת אנתם

3   אתנצחן֯ן] והנדרוא עבדו לפקיד֯ן֯א֯ זי֯ן֯לי עד מנדת ן֯בניא אלך יהי֯ן֯תה
עלי בבא֯ל כן עב֯ן֯דרן]

4   כזי לי תחדון אף ה֯ן֯א֯ן] שנ֯ן שני֯א זי בנ֯א֯ זן֯ך . . . . .] לא כשר אף
אחתבס֯תי פקידא ן֯ז֯ילי]

5 או אחוהי או ברה יאתה עלי בבאל עם מנדתא

B

6 מן ורונהי על נחןתחןוןרן וחנןדֹסירֹםן פןק ....[

From Varuvahya to Nakhthor, Kendasirma and his associates:

I have registered a complaint here to Arshama concerning my steward Ahatubasti, that he is not bringing me any of the [rent]. [. . .] is being brought to [Babylon].

Now you are to give my steward strict instructions to bring the rent [of those estates] to me in Babylon. Do it to please me! As you know, [the finances of] that estate have not been in order[5] for many years.

Furthermore, [my] steward Ahatubasti or his brother or his son is to come to me in Babylon with the rent.

Address: From Varuvahya to Nakhthor, Hendasirma [*sic*] [. . . .]

Commission for a Sculptor

46. AD 9 (Bodleian Pell. Aram. III)
(Provenance Unknown, Written from Babylon or Susa; late fifth century B.C.E.)

A

1 מן ארשם על נחתחור כנזסרם וכנותה וכעת חנזןנןי שמה
פתכרכר עלין[מֹא]ן זילי זי בנסרו היתי שושן זך פתפא הב

2 לה כאחרנֹן ֹולנשי ֹולנשי ֹביתהֹ נרד בדיכרן]זֹיֹ[לי ויעבד פתכרן זי פרש
[. . . . .] יֹהוֹוֹן וֹןיֹעֹן[בד פתכרֹ סוסה עם רכבה לקבל זי קדמן עבד
קד]מֹ[ןֹיֹ

3 ופתכרן אחרנן והושרו יהיתו עלי אֹפריע לעבק ול[עב]ק ארתוהי ידע
טעמ[א זנ]ה רשת ספרא

B

4 מן ארשם / על / נחתחור / פֿקֿי[נ]דא כֿנֿזֿסֿר[ם וֹ]כֿנֿוֹ[חתה המֿ]נֿרכֿ[ר]יא זי
במצרין

5 [עֿלֿ . .]

6 [. . . .]

7 [. . . .]

8 [. . . .]

9 ⟨Demotic⟩

From Arshama to Nakhthor, Kenzasirma and his associates.
Concerning: Hinzanay,[6] a sculptor and a servant of mine, whom Bagasrava
brought to Susa.

Issue rations to him and his household, the same as those given to the other
artisans[7] on my staff.

He is to make statues of a horseman [. . .]. They should be [. . .]. And
he is to make a statue of a horse with its rider, just as he did previously for
me, and other statues. Have them sent to me just as soon as you can!

Artavahya has been informed of this order.

Rashta

Scribe

Address: From Arshama to Nakhthor the steward, Kenzasirma and his associates
the accountants in Egypt.   ·

[*Fragments of four illegible short lines.*]

Demotic: Hotephep.

═══════════════ **Complaints** ═══════════════

47. AD 12 (Bodleian Pell. Aram. XIV)
(Provenance Unknown, Written from Babylon or Susa; late fifth century B.C.E.)

A

1 מן ורפש על נחתחור וכעת מספת [פֿ]קֿידא זי לי ֿשלח עליֿ כן / אמר

ככל לם אגרת מן ארשם יהבתׄ

2   על [פׄסׄמשׄ]ך בר עחחפי למנתן חלכין [נברן 5ׄ] וככל[. . . .] לי
חלכין   5   כל נברן [10]

3   אחר חלכיא נברן   5   שאל מן [נחתׄ]חור ולא יׄהׄב   /   לי כעת ורׄפש [כׄ]ן
אמר הא אנת

4   חזי אגרת ארשם זי היתיו   /   על פׄסמשׄך על חלכיא   /   זי מלכו   /   לי נברן
5 [. . . .] הב למספת

5   חלכנ[י]א אלך   5   שטר   /   מן זי יהבו בכבאל נברן   5   אף   /   קבילה שלח
עליך חמרא לם

6   זי בׄפׄרׄם ועבור ארקתא כלא נחתחורׄ לקח   /   עבד לנפשה כעת חמרא
עבורא ומנד[עׄם]

7   אחרן זי לקחת כלא התב   /   הב למספת יעבד על ביתא זילי למה כזי תאתה
בזנה

8   מה זי לקחת זיני תשלם ותשתאל על   /   זנה אף מספת שלח נרדא לם זי
מראתי

9   כתש ונכמן לקח   /   מנה כעת אנת ונרדא זילי עבידה לא אית לך ומה זי

B★

10   לקחת [נׄכׄסׄן] מׄן   /   נרדא התב הב   /   להם

11   כנ[וׄן] כזי מספת קבילה תובא לא ישלח

12   ע[ל]יך[ן]

C

13   מׄן ורפש עׄל [נחׄ]תחונׄר פקידא זי ב[מׄ]צׄרׄיׄן

14   על [. . . .]

15   זי [. . . . .]

16   מספת [. . . .]

17   [. . . . .]

★ Written sideways along the right margin.

From Varfish to Nakhthor:
My steward Masapata has sent me word as follows:

> A letter from Arshama was delivered to Psamshek son of Ahhapi in Babylon
> instructing him to give me five Cilician men. He gave me five additional
> Cilicians in Babylon—[ten] men in all.
>
> Later, Nakhthor was asked for the other five Cilician men, but he did not
> give them to me.

Now I, Varfish declare:

You are to follow the instructions in the letter of Arshama which was delivered
to Psamshek concerning the five Cilician men. [You are to] give Masapata
those five Cilicians over and above the five men given to him in Babylon.

On another matter, he has sent me a complaint against you:

> Nakhthor has misappropriated the Papremis[8] wine and all the field grain.[9]

The wine, the grain and anything else you took—give it all back to Masapata.
He is to make them over to my estate. Otherwise, when you come here, you
will pay damages for what you took and will be punished for this.

On still another matter, Masapata has sent word:

> He has beaten up my lady's household staff and has taken property from her.

You are to have nothing whatever to do with my household staff.[10] And as
for the property you took from the staff, give it back to them, so that Masapata
doesn't have to send another complaint [against you].

Address: From Varfish to Nakhthor [the steward in] Egypt.
Docket: Concerning [. . .] which [. . .] Masapata [. . .].

========= **Complaint of Unsatisfactory Goods** =========

48. AD 13 (Bodleian Pell. Aram. X)
(Provenance Unknown, Written from Babylon or Susa;
late fifth century B.C.E.)

A

1   מן ארן[ת]חן[ין] על נחתחור שלם ושררת שניא הושרת לך וכע֗נת אנ[ת]
[. . . .] אתנצח[ן]

2 [. . . . .] כֹֿן עבד כוי לאלהיא ולארשם תחֹן֯דִי֯ן] אף זי הושרת [. . . .]

עלי ביד אנאֹן [. . . . . . .]

3 [. . . . .] תחדו כתן / 1 גֹלֹדי תולע 2 זך היתי עלי להן לא

[. . . .] אנת הושרת וֹן [. . . .]

4 [. . . . .]סרת ואנה לֿ[אֹן] חדית אנת שגיא פתן֯סֹ]חתו לי ומנן . . .

[תֹמֹן . .]

5 [. . . . . . .] אלהיא שלם ישמו לך

B

6 מן ארתחי על נחתחור

From Artahaya to Nakhthor:

I send you greetings and best wishes for your good health.

You should be careful [. . .]. Do this so that you may please the gods and Arshama.

Now the shipment you sent [has been delivered] to me by Ana[-. . . .] a tunic, and two purple skins were delivered to me, but [I am] not [satisfied with them]. You have shipped [me things I don't need,] and I am not pleased.

You have always given me excellent service[11] and [. . .]. May the gods grant you good health!

Address: From Artahaya to Nakhthor.

═══════════════ **A Boatyard Work Order** ═══════════════

49. AP 26 (Cairo, Eg. Mus. Pap. 3432 = J. 43469)
(Elephantine: January 11, 411 B.C.E.)

A

1 מן ארשם על וחפרעמחי וכעת בלאֹן] . . . . [. . . .]

2 עלין מתרדת נופתא לם כן אמר פסמסניֹ]ת [. . . .]

3 כרכיא כן אמרו ספינתא זי מהחסנן אנֿחֹנֿה עדן הוה אופשרה למעֹנֿבד

[. . . . . .]

4 יתנגד על [ת]בלא וישתלח על המרכריא זי גנזא המו עם פרמנכר[יא
[..........

5 יחוו ואופכרתה יעבדו וישתלח על מן זי הוה אשרנא הנדונה ואחרן זי
[......]

6 ינתנו ולעבק אופשרה יתעבד ואחרן זי מני שליח עליהם על זנא שלחו
וכן [אמרו...... על]

7 חלא זי לקבל בן[י]רתא בן .....]ה מֹתֹרֹדֹת נופתא החוין ספינתא נחוי
זי ביד פסמסנית [......]

8 כל תרין נופתֹ[י]̂א זי כרכיא נגידה על תבלא ואנחנה החוין לשמשלך
וכנותה פרמנכריא שמו ב[ר]

9 כנופי סגן נגריא ספיתכן וכן אמרו עדן הוה אופֹשֹׁנ[רן]ֹה למעבד זנה
אשרנא זי אפיתי אופשרה

10 למעבד עקי ארז ואר חדתן טף אמן עשרה שים [ל]בטק אמן תמנין
בפשכן תלתה בנו סגנן אמן עשרה

11 ותרין שף עשרה וחמשה חד [ל]אמן עשרן סעבל אמן שבען חנן לבטנא
תלתה קלעם לק[ו]מתא חד

12 עקי חלא אמן שתן פחטמוני לפערער חד לאמן תרין אפסי תחת חלא
חמשא מסמרי נחש ופרזל

13 מאתין עקי ארז לובר חסין תמים אמן עשרן כלא יהיתה חליפתהם
לובר ותבירן על גנזא עזלי

14 כתן עבין כרשן מאה ותמנין רקען כרשן מאתין וחמשן עקי ארז חדתן
חנן תרין לחד אמן חמשה

15 פשכן תלתה בפשכן תלתה לחלא מסמרי נחש מאה וחמשן לחד פשכן תלתה
מאתין שבען וחמשה

16 לחד צבען עשרה חד מסמרין ארבע מאה עשרן וחמשה טסן זי נחש אמן
עשרן מסמריהם מאתין

B

17 עקי ארז לובר דשות מצן כנכר חד מנן עשרה כלא הוספה
כברי כרשן עשרה ולהנדונה זרניך כרשן מאה

18 ויהוספון על עקיא זי יתיהב על טף בארכא לחד פשכן תלתה חפוש ועל
פתיא ועביא צבען תרין ועל

19 שים בארכא לחד פשכן תלתה חפוש ועל פתיא צבען תרין ועל שף
 וחנניא בארכא לחד פשך חד ועל

20 סעבל עקי חלא דרי תמים בארכא לחד פשכן תלתה חפוש ועל פתיא צבע
חד עזלי כתנא רקעתא

21 זרניכא כבריתא במתקלת פרם יתיהב ישתלח לם אשרנא זנה יתיהב עֿל /
יד שמו בר כנופי סגן

22 נגריא ספיתכן לעינין אופשר ספינתא זך ולעבק יעבד כזי שים טעם
כעת ארשם כן אמר אנת עבד

23 לקבל זנה זי המרכריא אמרן כזי שים טעם עניני ספרא בעל טעם
נבועקב כתב

24 וחפרעמחי [. . . .] יתיהֿב לתוכֿה בֿלֿ[. . ל . . . .] כותה
[. . . .] . . .

25 כזי שים טעם [. . . .]לֿ כתב

26 ‹Demotic›

27 מן ארשם זי במצֿ[ןרין על וחפרעמחי . . . . [

28 נבועקב ספרא ב 13 [לֿ]טבת שנת 12 דריו[הוש מלכא]

From Arshama to Wahpremahi.

Bel-[. . .[12] the . . . and . . . the . . . have sent me word as follows: . . .] to us. Mithradata the boatman has sent us word as follows:

Psamsineith [son of . . . and . . . son of . . . , the two] Carian [boatmen], have reported to me: "It is time to make repairs[13] on the boat we hold."[14] [We sent word to Arshama and he said to us as follows:]

> Let it be brought into dry dock, and let word be sent to the treasury accountants. They and the estimators(?) [. . .] are to be shown [the boat], and should make an estimate(?). Let word be sent to whomever is in charge that they should supply [whatever] materials, paint, etc., [are required], and that the repairs, etc., ordered by me should be made immediately.

They sent back word [as follows:

> *We had it drawn up on*] the sand opposite the fortress [. . .], and Mithradata the boatman showed the boat to us. We report that it was brought into dry dock by Psamsineith and [. . .], the two Carian boatmen. We showed it to Shamash-shillek and his associates the estimators(?), and Shamaw son of Kanufi the master boatwright(?), and they said as follows: "It is time to make repairs(?)."

Following is a list of materials needed(?) for repairs(?).

New Cedar and . . .-wood:

. . . ⟨tp⟩ *	10 cubits
. . . ⟨šym⟩ for . . .	80 cubits by 3 handbreadths
(including . . .'s	12 cubits)
. . . ⟨šp⟩'s	15, each 20 cubits long
. . . ⟨s'bl⟩ -wood	70 cubits
. . . ⟨ḥnn⟩'s for the hold	3
. . . for the mast[15]	1

Wood for the Gunwale:

Mooring-post for the prow(?)	1, two cubits long
Stanchions(?) under the gunwale	5

Bronze and Iron Nails:	200

Strong Well-Seasoned(?) Cedar:

Paneling	20 cubits

Note: For all of the above, he should bring the old(?) and broken materials being replaced to the treasury.

Canvas:	180 *karsh* by weight
Metal Plating(?):	250 *karsh*

New Cedar:

. . .'s	2, each 5 cubits long, 3 x 3 handbreadths

Bronze Nails for the Gunwale	150, 3 handbreadths each
	275, 10 fingerbreadths each
	Total nails: 425

Bronze Plating:	20 cubits + 200 nails for it

Well-Seasoned(?) . . .-Cedar:

. . .	1 talent, 1 *mina*

Miscellaneous:

Sulfur	10 *karsh*
Arsenic for paint	100 *karsh*

To be added to the lumber for delivery:

Onto the . . . ⟨tp⟩ :	length, 3 handbreadths overcut(?)
	width and thickness, 2 fingerbreadths
Onto the . . . ⟨šym⟩ :	length, 3 handbreadths overcut(?)
	width, 2 fingerbreadths

* A sign such as ⟨tp⟩ , etc., indicates consonants of untranslatable words.

Onto each . . . ⟨*šp*⟩
and . . . ⟨*ḥnn*⟩ :   length, 1 handbreadth
Onto the . . . ⟨*s'bl*⟩ , the wood
for the gunwale(?) and
the panel sections, (to
each of the above):   length, 3 handbreadths overcut(?)
                       width, 1 fingerbreadth

Note: The canvas, the plating, the arsenic and the sulfur should be given according to the Persian weight.[16]

Send word: These materials are to be handed over to Kanufi, chief carpenter and master boatwright(?), so the boat can be repaired immediately, as ordered.

Now I, Arshama, declare: Follow the instructions of the accountants, as ordered!

                       Anani the scribe, Chancellor
                       Nabuaqab wrote it

Additional notations: Wahpremahi [. . .] to be given [. . .] accordingly [. . .] as ordered. [. . .] wrote. ⟨Demotic⟩ : Sasobek wrote [. . .] The boat [. . .].

Address: From Arshama in Egypt [to Wahpremahi].
Scribe and date: Nabuaqab, scribe, thirteenth of Tebeth, twelfth year of [King] Darius.

Notes

1. A variant or misspelling of the Persian name "Artavant."
2. For this translation, see Hinz 1973: 40.
3. Evidently a Persian loanword meaning "food-warden" (Hinz 1973: 42). The person in question is administrator of a tenant farm.
4. Though the letter is addressed to a single administrator, the pronouns here are plural.
5. Or, "That estate has not produced its proper [rent] for many years."
6. The reading and derivation of the name are uncertain.
7. Or "stonecutters" (Grelot 1972: 318c).
8. The word has been identified with "Papremis" (a Delta town whose exact location is unknown) mentioned in Herodotus 2.59, 63, 71, 165 (Grelot 1972: 74c). It may refer to a variety of wine, or simply to the place where it was stored.
9. Possibly "Seed grain."

10. Literally, "Now you and my household staff—there is no business!"

11. The literal sense seems to be, "You are very praiseworthy [a Persian loanword of uncertain meaning] to me," but the writer appears to contrast former good service with the present complaint.

12. Perhaps "Bel-iddin" or another common Akkadian name of the period.

13. Or "to make a . . . for the boat we hold." The meaning of the key word, apparently a Persian loan, is not known.

14. The term refers to property held in tenure, and is commonly used of lands.

15. Or "bow."

16. The Egyptian and Persian system of weights did not exactly correspond. See *karsh* in the glossary.

VI

A Hebrew
Judicial Petition

============ Introduction ============

Around 628 B.C.E., young king Josiah of Judah launched his famous religious and political reform, described in 2 Kings 22–23 (cf. 2 Chronicles 34–35). This period provides the historical background of a unique letter of petition (No. 50). Discovered in 1960 by Israeli archaeologists excavating a small Iron Age fortress near Yavneh-Yam between Jaffa and Ashdod (the site has since been named Mezad Hashavyahu), it is a palm-sized ostracon composed in reasonably good classical Hebrew. Whether or not it was written by a trained scribe is a matter of some debate. Most of the characters are written legibly and clearly, though the fourteen lines of script meander somewhat clumsily.

The petitioner at whose dictation the letter was written—it is doubtful he wrote it himself—is a poor farm laborer, perhaps a corvée worker doing forced labor on state-owned lands (Yeivin 1962: 8–10; Pardee 1982: 24). The addressee is an unnamed person in a position of authority. The Hebrew word translated "commander" is rather unspecific and can be used of various kinds of civil and military authorities. Probably the local military governor is meant.

The laborer claims that his outer garment has been unjustly appropriated by a certain Hoshayahu. Israel's oldest legal traditions forbid a creditor to take a garment in pledge and keep it overnight (Exod 22:25–26 [Eng. 22:26–27]). In Deuteronomy, the same prohibition is followed by an injunction "not to oppress the hired servant who is poor and needy" (Deut 24:12–15; cf. v. 17). Amos refers to a breach of this ancient commandment in listing the sins of the Israelites of his day (Amos 2:8). Although Hoshayahu's offense was not precisely the same as the act forbidden in Exodus, since there is no suggestion in the letter that the garment was taken in pledge for a loan, it is clear

96

that his action was contrary to the spirit of Torah and prophets alike. The document allows a fleeting glimpse of rural Israel in the time of the reformer king: a poor laborer, harvesters laboring in the heat of the day, an oppressive foreman, an ancient custom flouted, a humble appeal to the nearest person with the power to redress the wrong.

A Judicial Petition

50. Mezad Hashavyahu Ostracon (IM 60–67)
(Near Yavneh-Yam; reign of Josiah)

1   ישמע אדני . השר

2   את דבר עבדה . עבדך

3   קצר . היה עבדך . בח-

4   צראסם . ויקצר עבדך

5   ויכל ואסם כימם . לפני שב-

6   ת כאשר כל]ע[בדך את קצר וא-

7   סם כימם ויבא . הושעיהו בן שב-

8   י . ויקח . את בגד עבדך כאשר כלת

9   את קצרי זא ימם לקח את בגד עבדך

10 וכל אחי . יענו לי . הקצרם אתי בחם

11 הֹשֶֹמשׁ אחי . יענו לי אמן נקתי . מא-

12]שם השב נא את[בגדי ואם לא . לשר להש-

13]ב את בגד עֹבֹ]דך ותתֹ]ן אלו . רח-

14]מם והש[בֹת אֹת]בגד ע[בדך ולא תדהם] . . [

15]. . . . . [

May my lord, the commander[1] hear the appeal of his servant.

Your servant is a reaper working in Hazar-asam. Your servant finished his harvest and stored it a few days before stopping.[2] After your servant had finished storing the harvest a few days ago, Hoshayahu son of Shobay came and took your servant's garment.

All my companions who were harvesting with me in the heat of the [sun] will testify for me. They will testify that what I have said is true. I am innocent of any [offense.]

[So please return] my garment. If the commander does not consider it his obligation to have [your servant's garment] sent back, [do] it out of pity! You must not remain silent [when your servant is without his garment.]

Notes

1. Or "governor."
2. Or "before Sabbath."

VII

Judean Military-Administrative Letters from Arad and Lachish

This chapter contains two collections of military letters in Hebrew from the last days of the Judean monarchy. Originating in Arad, the letters in the first group (Nos. 51–60) date mostly to around 597 B.C.E. The second group, from Lachish (Nos. 61–67), is probably to be dated about eight years later. These letters, together with the biblical accounts of the campaigns of Nebuchadrezzar and the Babylonian Chronicle (Wiseman 1956), give us more thorough documentation of these years than for any comparable period in ancient Israel's history.

By the late seventh century, the Neo-Assyrian empire was on the verge of collapse. Nineveh fell in 612 to a coalition of Babylonians and Medes. A few Assyrian troops under Ashur-uballit II resisted for three more years, but by 609, the year of Josiah's death (2 Kgs 23:29; 2 Chr 35:20–24), the last vestiges of Assyrian power had been crushed. For the next half century, the new imperial power in Mesopotamia was to be Babylonia.

In Judah, Josiah's son Jehoahaz (Shallum) was crowned in 609 in his father's place. But the Egyptian Pharaoh Necho (609–594), ever eager to intervene in Judean affairs, replaced him with his brother Jehoiakim (also called Eliakim [609–598]; see 2 Kgs 23:31–35), and for several years Egypt was the power behind the Judean throne. Egyptian troops remained in Syria, while the Babylonians under King Nabopolassar and young Prince Nebuchadrezzar consolidated their power closer home.

In 605 Nebuchadrezzar brought his armies back to Syria and met the Egyptians head on, dealing them a decisive defeat at Carchemish, and again near Hamath. In August, he returned home to assume the throne on the death of his father, but by late the next year he was back, leading his forces down the Philistine coast (cf. Jeremiah 47 and the Babylonian Chronicle). King Adon's futile appeal to Egypt for assistance (No. 2) dates from this time. Meanwhile, Jehoiakim switched his allegiance from Egypt to Babylonia.

In the winter of 601–600, Nebuchadrezzar tried to invade Egypt, but met such stiff resistance that he was compelled to draw back to Babylonia to regroup, prompting Jehoiakim to rebel. For three years, until Nebuchadrezzar was able to return to the west, he kept the Judeans off balance by harassing them with armed bands of Moabites, Ammonites, and Arameans, supported by a few Babylonian army units still in the area. In the eastern Negeb, cross-border raids from Edom became more and more common (Nos. 53–54).

In December 598 the expected Babylonian retribution came, and Jerusalem was besieged. Jehoiakim died suddenly, either in defense of the city or at the hands of an assassin. His young son Jehoiachin surrendered in March 597, and along with many of the leading people in the land, was carried away to Babylonia.

The following years were chaotic, with successive attempts by Judean nationalists to gain independence and punitive measures by the Babylonians to reassert their authority. Around 589, Judah rebelled again, hoping for support from Egypt, where Hophra (Apries, 589–570) had just ascended the throne.

Once more the Babylonians marched on Judah and blockaded Jerusalem (in early 588 or a year later). Jerusalem was cut off for eighteen months, with only one brief respite when the Babylonians had to withdraw to repel an Egyptian force from the south. One by one the other fortifications in Judah were taken, Lachish and Azekah being the last to hold out. By this time, Jerusalem had been reduced to desperate straits by famine, and in July 587 the Babylonians breached the city wall. Jerusalem was captured, looted, and razed. Top officials were executed, and many more were taken away by their conquerors. The Babylonian exile had begun.

Arad, find-site of the first group of letters in this chapter, was a city in the eastern Negeb, roughly halfway between Beersheba and the Dead Sea, near the modern town of the same name. The oldest remains of the settlement date from the Early Bronze Age. During the Israelite monarchy, Arad's border location, astride the trails leading up the wadis from Edom into southern Judah, gave it particular strategic importance. A stone fortification tower, some fifty meters square, was erected during the time of the United Monarchy. Over succeeding centuries this citadel was repeatedly destroyed and rebuilt, down to the time of the Romans. Israeli and American archaeologists digging at Arad from 1962 to 1967 uncovered twelve strata from the Israelite period and later.

In the late monarchic period, the time of these letters, Arad was a fortified supply depot. Staple foods were stockpiled and sent on demand to Judean army units stationed throughout the region. It also served as a troop transit point (see No. 53). Archaeological evidence indicates that the fortress fell temporarily into Egyptian hands in 609. The Egyptians confiscated the supplies in the warehouse, then burned the citadel. Two inventories of foodstuffs, one in hieratic Egyptian, the other in Hebrew, probably date from this incident (Aharoni 1981: 61–64).

Shortly thereafter, probably in 604, when Babylonia was on the move and the Egyptians no longer could maintain their influence, the fort was rebuilt by Judah on the same general plan as before. The new citadel stood only about a decade. In 597, while

Nebuchadrezzar's army was invading Judah from the north, the fortress was captured and destroyed again, apparently by raiders from Edom.

The excavators of Arad found over a hundred Hebrew inscriptions and ostraca, most of them fragmentary, dating from the ninth to the early sixth century. Twenty-one or twenty-two ostraca can be identified as letters, of which nine are included here. There are unresolved questions concerning stratigraphy and dating (Aharoni 1981: 9, 70–74; Holladay 1976; 275, 281 n. 26; Pardee 1978b: n. 144; 1982: 28), but most of the letters were written between the beginning of Josiah's reign and the final capture of Jerusalem by Babylonia. Nos. 53–60 are generally dated to early 597, just before Jehoiachin surrendered Jerusalem. No. 52, found on the surface, seems slightly earlier. No. 51 is still earlier, going back to the latter years of Manasseh (687/686–642), the time of Amon (642–640), or the earlier years of Josiah (640–609).

Two distinct types of letters are found at Arad. First, there is official military correspondence — orders and reports concerning such matters as troop disposition (No. 53) and intelligence (No. 51; see also Nos. 52 and 54). Second, there are notes concerning the issue and dispatch of rations (Nos. 55–60).

A recurrent motif is the threat from Edom. No. 51 alludes to intelligence reports from Edom. No. 53 is an urgent order from the king (Jehoiakim or Jehoiachin) to reinforce the Judean garrison at nearby Ramat-Negeb (Horvat Uza?; see Josh 19:8; 1 Sam 30:27) against the Edomites (Aharoni 1981: 146–48; otherwise Lemaire 1977: 192). No. 52 is apparently a letter from a new king of Judah, possibly Jehoahaz or Jehoiakim.

Nos. 55–60 are requisitions from commanders in other locations, authorizing the release and transport of grain, flour, dough, bread, wine, vinegar, and olive oil, with occasional appended notes on other topics (see Nos. 56–58). One contains a cryptic allusion to a man who has taken up residence (possibly asylum) in the temple at Jerusalem (No. 55), the only known extrabiblical reference to the first temple. There are frequent references to "Greeks" (Hebrew *kittiyyîm*, a word used centuries later at Qumran to refer to Romans), either Greek mercenaries in the service of Judah or itinerant middlemen who distributed supplies.

The person most often named in the requisitions is Elyashib ben Eshyahu, chief supply officer at Arad. Modern writers often refer to him as commander of the fortress, but it is not certain that his responsibilities went beyond those of a quartermaster. Letters 55–60 were found in the ruins of Elyashib's office. Three seals from a slightly earlier stratum and several other documents also bear his name. Elyashib evidently held his post before the citadel was taken by Egypt in 609, and returned to his command when it was rebuilt in 604.

The letters from Lachish (Nos. 61–67) provide a fragmentary but unparalleled picture of the day-to-day concerns of a Judean officer on the eve of the Babylonian attack in 587. They also reflect the factionalism and political maneuvering in the capital at the time.

Lachish is situated in the Judean Shephelah, midway along an ancient road leading from Ashkelon on the coast to Hebron. Like Arad, Lachish was a royal fortress built on the ruins of a more ancient town. But whereas Arad was a fortified storehouse with a citadel of no great size, Lachish was an immense, walled bastion, the greatest fortified city in Judah after Jerusalem.

Long before these letters were written, when Sennacherib of Assyria invaded Judah in 701, Lachish had played a key role in the defense of the nation. At that time, the city fell only after a protracted siege and a massed assault by Assyrian heavy armor. Sennacherib had his propaganda artists depict the siege on stone reliefs, which he displayed in his palace at Nineveh. The evident pride the Assyrian monarch took in the capture of Lachish indicates just how difficult a feat it was.

When Nebuchadrezzar besieged Jerusalem in early 588/587, Lachish once again played a significant role in the defense of Judah. According to Jer 34:6–7, it was one of the last two fortresses to fall before the capital itself.

The site of Lachish, modern Tell ed-Duweir, was excavated in the 1930s. A collection of Hebrew ostraca, mostly letters, was unearthed in the remains of the level destroyed in 587/586. Sixteen were found in a single room, thought to be a guard room, just inside the main entry gate at the southwest corner of the city wall.

Of the seven letters translated here, six are from the guard room. No. 65 was found under the surface of a later roadway, but is contemporary with the other six. Their content is varied, but the letters are similar in style and tone, often using variants of the same formulas and clichés. The epistolary style is rather different from that of the Arad letters, suggesting writers trained in two different scribal traditions.

The Lachish letters were written over a very short span of time. Nos. 61 and 64 are actually written on pieces of the same broken pot. The most likely date is the summer of 588/587. The Babylonian invasion is imminent, but there is no hint that the Chaldean armies are actually in the land. On the contrary, it is still possible to travel unimpeded from Lachish to Jerusalem ("the city," No. 63), to Egypt (No. 62), and to the countryside for harvest (No. 66; on the dating see Pardee 1982: 77, 98).

Several thorny issues relating to the interpretation of these letters remain unresolved. Without entering into the debates, I simply state the assumptions made here: (1) Tell ed-Duweir is ancient Lachish; (2) these ostraca are copies or drafts of letters sent from (not to) Lachish (see Yadin 1984); (3) the addressee, Yaush, named only in Nos. 61, 62, and 64, is the intended recipient of most or all of the other letters; (4) Yaush is probably located in Jerusalem; (5) Hoshayahu, named as the sender of No. 62, is the author of the entire collection. These assumptions provide a coherent framework in which to read the letters.

Hoshayahu's exact position at Lachish is not certain, but his primary responsibilities relate to communication, in particular the collection and evaluation of military intelligence. He receives written reports from Jerusalem and elsewhere, which he sometimes returns without comment (No. 66), and sometimes subjects to a cutting analysis, evaluating their political and military implications (No. 64). In turn, he reports on matters which he presumes are not known to his superior in Jerusalem (No. 62). He also reports back on the execution of previous orders (No. 63; cf. 61), and once requests orders when none have been received (No. 67). Military couriers appear to have carried messages to and from the capital at least once daily.

The allusion to a signal fire in No. 63 evidently refers to a military communications system. It has recently been suggested that the Lachish light was part of a comprehensive network of signal beacons linking the fortresses of the Judean Shephelah with Jerusalem (Mazar 1981). Given the probable date of the letters, the phrase "We cannot see Azekah" is not, as some interpreters have held, a reference to the fall of that city, but is to be understood in the context of testing the signal system and training soldiers to its use prior to the arrival of the invasion forces.

The Lachish letters reflect the personality of their author more clearly than any other

group in this collection. Hoshayahu comes across as a crusty, blunt-speaking, profes-
sional soldier, confident of his own ability and utterly tactless in the face of authority.
He is given to emotional outbursts, sarcasm, and heavy-handed irony. This is especially
evident in his repeated use of the phrase "I am nothing but a dog." The phrase is a
traditional formula of self-abasement in the presence of greater authority. But
Hoshayahu, although outranked by Yaush ("my lord"), is not in the least cowed by
his superior, as is clear from his angry outburst when Yaush impugns his ability to
read (No. 62). Hoshayahu's insubordinate criticism of royal officials in Jerusalem,
possibly all the way up to the king himself (No. 64), is reminiscent of the complaints
of many a line officer in later times, convinced that the politicians are ruining the conduct
of the war. Hoshayahu and Yaush appear as "hardliners" who want to avoid any state-
ments by national leaders that would undermine troop morale.

══════ A Report from Edom ══════

51. Arad 40 (IM 67–631)
(Second half of seventh century B.C.E.)

1   בנכם . גמר[יהו] ונח-

2   מיהו . שלחו לשלם]

3   מלכיהו ברכתך ליהוה]

4   ועת . הטה [ע]בדך [ל]בה

5   אל . אשר אמ]רת וכתבת]י

6   אל אדני [את כל אשר ר-]

7   צה . האיש [ואשיהו ב-]

8   א . מאתך . והאיש] לא נתן ל[-]

9   הם . והן . ידעתה [המכתבם מ-]

10   אדם . נתתם לאדנ]י בטרם י-[]

11   רד ים . ונא]שי[ן]הו . לן [כביתי]

12   והא . המכתב . בקש [ולא נתת-]

13   י . ידע . מלך . יהוד]ה כי אי-[]

14   ננו . יכלם . לשלח . את הן...] וז-[]

15   את הרעה אש[ר] אד]ם עשתה]

Your son Gemar[yahu] and Nehemyahu send [greetings] to Malkiyahu.
I bless [you by YHWH].

Your servant has applied himself to what you ordered. [I am] writing to my lord [everything that] the man wanted.

[Eshyahu has] come from you, but [he has not given] them any men. You know [the reports from] Edom. I sent them to [my lord [before] evening. Eshyahu is staying [in my house]. He tried to obtain the report, [but I would not give it to him].

The king of Judah should be told [that] we [are unable] to send [. . .],[1] [This is] the evil which the Edomites [have done].

A Royal Fragment

52. Arad 88 (Arad Excav. Reg. No. 7904/1)
(609 B.C.E. [?])

1   אני . מלכתי . בכ]ל . . . . . [
2   אמץ זרע . ו]ן . . . . . [
3   מלך . מצרים . ל]ן . . . . . [

I have become king in all . . . . Be strong and . . . . the king of Egypt to . . . .

Orders from the King

53. Arad 24 (IM 72–121)
(597 B.C.E.)

A

1   אל[. . . . .]
2   אלישב] . . . .[
3   לס] . . . .[מלך] . [במ] . . . . . .[
4   ] . . . .[חיל] . . . .[
5   ] . . . .[כס] . . . .[
6   ] . . . .[עבד] . . . .[
7   ] . . . .[ט] . . . . .[ר] . . . .[
8   ] . . . .[וע] . . . .[

9   [. . . . . .][וכ][. . . . .]

10   [. . . . .]

11   [. . . . .]

B

12   מערד 50 ומקינ]ה[. . . . . .]

13   ה . ושלחתם . אתם . רמתנגנ]ב בי-]

14   ד . מלכיהו בן קרבאור והב-

15   קידם . על . יד אלישע בן ירמי-

16   הו ברמתנגנב . פן . יקרה . את ה-

17   עיר . דבר . ודבר המלך אתכם

18   בנבשכם . הנה שלחתי להעיד

19   בכם . הים . האנשם את . אליש-

20   ע . פן . תבא . אדם . שמה

To [. . .] Elyashib [. . .].

[. . .] king [. . .] army [. . .] servant [. . .].

[. . .] fifty from Arad, and [. . .] from Qinah [. . .]. Send them to Ramat-Negeb [under] the command of Malkiyahu son of Qerabur. He is to hand them over to Elisha son of Yirmeyahu at Ramat-Negeb, so that nothing will happen to the city.

This is an order from the king—a life and death matter for you. I am sending you this message to warn you now: these men *must* be with Elisha in case the Edomites come!

54. Arad 21 (IM 72–126)
(597 B.C.E.)

1   בנד . יהוכל . שלח . לשלם . גדליהו]בן[

2   אליאר . ולשלם . ביתך ברכתך לן]יהו-]

3   ה . ועת . הן . עשה אדני . [. . . . . .]

4   [. . . . . . .]י[שלם . יהוה . לאדנ]י . . . . [

5   [. . . . .]אדם[.]חיה]וה . . . .]

6   [. . . . .] . . . .]הן[. . . .]עת[. . . . .]

7 　[. . . . .]　ר‏[שא לכו‏](. . . . .]
8 　[. . . .]　םאו　.　דו‏[ע‏](. . . . .]
9 　[. . . . .]‏[שא‏](. . . . .]
10 　[. . . .]‏[חל‏](. . . . .]

Your son Yehukal sends greetings to Gedalyahu [son of] Elyair and your household!

I bless you by [YHWH].

If my lord has done [. . .], may YHWH reward [my] lord [. . .]. [. . .] Edom [. . .] by God [. . .] whatever [. . .] and if [there is?] still [. . .].

══════════ **Rations and Other Matters** ══════════

55. Arad 18 (IM 67–669)
(597 B.C.E.)

A

1　-‏ילא　.　ינדא לא
2　-‏שי הוהי　.　בש
3　תעו　.　ךמלשל לא
4　והירמשל　.　ןת
5　יסרקלו　.　√
6　-‏דלו　├　.　ןתת
7　-‏צ　.　רשא　.　רב
8　םלש　.　ינתו
9　הוהי　.　תיב

B

10　בשי　.　אה

To my lord Elyashib:

May YHWH bless you.

Issue Shemaryahu half a donkey-load of flour(?).[2] And give the Qerosite[3] a full donkey-load.

As for the matter about which you gave me orders — all is well.[4] He is staying in the temple of YHWH.[5]

56. Arad 1 (IM 67–713)
(597 B.C.E.)

1	אל . אלישב . ו-
2	עת . נתן לכתים
3	יין . ב׳ 3 ו-
4	כתב . שם / הים .
5	ומעוד . הקמח
6	הראשון . ת-
7	רכב . Ͱ 1 . קמח
8	לעשת . להם . ל-
9	חם . מיין .
10	האגנת . תתן

To Elyashib:

Issue the Greeks three large jugs[6] of wine and record the date. Have a donkey-load of flour loaded up for them to make bread with.

Take it from what's left of the old flour![7] Give them the wine from the craters.

57. Arad 2 (IM 67–625)
(597 B.C.E.)

1	אל . אלישב . ועת . נתן / ל-
2	כתים . ב׳ 2 יין . ל-
3	ארבעת / הימם ו-
4	300 לחם ו-
5	מלא . החמר . יין וה-
6	סבת מחר . אל / תאחר .
7	ואם . עוד . חמץ . ונת-
8	ת . להם .

To Elyashib:
Issue the Greeks two jugs of wine for the four days, three hundred loaves of bread, and a full donkey-load of wine.
Deliver tomorrow—don't be late! And if there is any vinegar, give them some.

58. Arad 3 (IM 67–623)
(597 B.C.E.)

A

1	אל . אלישב . ועת .
2	תן . מן . היין . 3 . ב׳ . ו-
3	צוך . חנניהו . על ב-
4	אר / שבע עם . משא צ-
5	מד . חמרם . וצררת
6	אתם . בצק . ו-
7	ספר . החטם והל-
8	חם ולקחת

B

9	אלכמ֗ן] . . . .[
10	רי[. . . . .]
11	ל[. . . . .]
12	ואדמם . ה]. . . . .[
13	] . . . .[
14	מ . .[. . . . .]

To Elyashib:
Issue three jugs of wine to bearer.
Hananyahu hereby orders you to Beersheba with a double donkey-load: Harness them up with a consignment of dough.[8]
Take inventory of the wheat, and count the loaves of bread. Take [. . .]. [*Rest illegible, except for the phrase* "and the Edomites."]

59. Arad 17 (IM 67–624)
(597 B.C.E.)

A

1 אל . נחם .]ו[עת ב-
2 א ביתה . אלישב .
3 בן אשיחו . ולקח-
4 ת . משם 1 . שמן ו-
5 שלח . ל] . .[. מהרה . ו-
6 חתם . אתה בח-
7 תמך

B

8 ב 24 לחדש נתן נחם ש-
9 מן ביד הכתי . 1

To Nahum:

   Go to the house of Elyashib son of Eshyahu. Get 1 measure[9] of oil from there, and send it immediately to . . . .[10] Seal it with your seal.

Endorsement (in another hand): On the twenty-fourth of the month, Nahum handed over the oil to the Greek for delivery: one measure.

60. Arad 16 (IM 67–990)
(597 B.C.E.)

1 אחך . חנניהו . שלח / לשל-
2 ם אלישב . ולשלם ביתך בר-
3 כתך ליהוה . ועת כצאתי
4 מביתך ושלחתי את
5 הנ]כ[סף 8 ש׳ לבני גאליהו .]ב-[
6 י]ד ע[זריהו ועת] . . . .[
7] . . .[אתך וה] . . . .[

8 ‏את כסף] [.....] ואם].....[
9 ‏[.] [.....] שלח] [.....]
10 ‏את נחם ולא תשלח ל] [.....]

[11–12 *Faint traces only*]

Your brother Hananyahu sends greetings to Elyashib and your household.
I bless you by YHWH!
When I left your house, I sent the money (eight shekels) to the sons of Geal-
yahu by Azaryahu, as well as the . . . with you (?). So . . . the money, and if . . . .
send . . . Nahum, but don't send . . . .

════════════ **Greetings to a Superior Officer** ════════════

61. Lachish 2 (BM 125 702)
(589 B.C.E.)

1 ‏אל אדני . יאוש ישמע
2 ‏יהוה . את אדני . ש]מעת[של-
3 ‏ם . עת / כים עת / כים מי . עבד-
4 ‏ך כלב כי . זכר אדני . את .
5 ‏[ע]בדה . יבכר . יהוה את א-
6 ‏[דנ]י דבר . אשר לא . ידעתה

To my lord Yaush.
May YHWH send you good news this very day!
I am nothing but a dog, why should you should think of me?[11] May YHWH
help you find out what you need to know!

══════ **Protest of Literacy, Troop Movements, etc.** ══════

62. Lachish 3 (IM 38–127)
(589 B.C.E.)

A

1   עבדך . הושעיהו . שלח . ל-
2   הגֹד לֹאֹדני יאוֹש . ישמע
3   יהוֹה אֹת אדני . שמעת . שלם
4   ושמעת . טֹב] .[וע]ת . הפקח
5   נֹא] . [את אזן] . [עבדך . לספר . אשר .
6   שלחתה] . [אל עבדך . אמש . כי . לב
7   עבדך דֹוה . מאז . שלחך . אל . עבד-
8   ך] . [וכי] . [אמר . אדני . לא . ידעתה .
9   קרא ספר חיהוה . אם . נסה . א-
10   יש לקרא לי . ספר לנצח . ונם .
11   כל ספר] . [אשר יבא . אלי] . [אם .
12   קראתי . אתה ועֹד . אתננהו
13   אל . מאומֹה ולעבדך . הגד .
14   לאמר . ירד שר . הצבא
15   כניהו בן אלנתן לבא .
16   מצרימה . ואת

B

17   הודויהו בן אחיהו ו-
18   אנשו שלח לקחת . מזה
19   וספר . טביהו עבד . המלך . הבא
20   אל . שלם . בן ידע . מאת . הנבא . לאמ-
21   ר . השמר . שלחה . עב<ד>ך . אל . אדני

A report from your servant Hoshayahu to my lord Yaush.
May **YHWH** send you good news and prosperity!

Now then, would you please explain to me what you meant by the letter you sent me last night? I've been in a state of shock ever since I got it. "Don't you know how to read a letter?" you said. By God,[12] nobody ever had to read *me* a letter! And when I get a letter, once I've read it, I can recite it back verbatim, word for word!

I have just received word that Commander Konayahu son of Elnatan has moved south to enter Egypt. He has sent to have Hodawyahu son of Ahiyahu and his men transferred from here.

I am sending a letter confiscated[13] by Tobyahu, the royal administrator. It was sent to Shallum son of Yada from the prophet, saying, "Beware!"

===== **Report on Signal-Fire and Other Matters** =====

63. Lachish 4 (IM 38–128)
(589 B.C.E.)

A

1   ישמע . יהו]ה את אדנ]י עת כים .

2   שמעת טב . ועת ככל אשר . שלח אדני.

3   כן . עשה . עבדך כתבתי על הדלת ככל .

4   אשר שלח]תה א[ן]לי . וכי . שלח א-

5   דני . על . דבר בית / הרפד אין . שם א-

6   דם וסמכיהו לקחה . שמעיהו ו-

7   יעלהו . העירה ועבדך . אינֹנ-

8   י] . [שֹלח שמה אֹת העד] הים]

B

9   כי אם . בתסבת . הבקר [י]בֹ[א]

10   וידע . כי אל . משאת לכש . נח-

11   נו שמרם . ככל . האתת . אשר נתן

12   אדני . כי לא ° נראה את עז-

13   קה

May YHWH send you good news this very day!

I have carried out all of your orders and have kept a written record of them: On the matter you spoke of regarding Beth-*hrpd*[14]: there is no one there. Regarding Semakyahu: Shemayahu has arrested him and had him taken up to the city. I cannot send the witness there today.

If you could be here during the morning watch, you would understand that we are tending the signal-fire of Lachish according to the code you gave us,[15] for we cannot see Azekah.

═══════════════════ **Morale** ═══════════════════

64. Lachish 6 (IM 38–129)
(589 B.C.E.)

1   אל אדני יאוש . ירא . יהוה א-

2   ת . אדני את העת הזה . שלם מי

3   עבדך . כלב כי . שלח . אדני א]ת ספ – [

4   ר המלך [ואת] ספרי השר]ם לאמ-]

5   ר קרא נא והנה . דברי . ה]שרם]

6   לא טבם לרפת ידיד] ולהש – [

7   קט . ידי הא]נשם . ..]ידע] . . . [

8   [. . . . .] אנכ]י [אדני הלא תכ-

9   תב אל]יהם] לא]מר למ]ה תעשו .

10   כזאת ו] . . . .] שלם] . . .] הל-

11   מלד] . . . . . .]ו] . [.]ד] . . [

12   [.]א] . . . .]חי . יהוה אלה-

13   יך כ]י מ]אז קרא עב-

14   דך את הספרם לא היה

15   לעב]דך [. . . . . . .]

To my lord Yaush.

May YHWH make this time a good one for you.

I am nothing but a dog, why should you should send me the letters from the king and the officials and ask me to read them?

What the officials say is not good. It will undermine your authority and the morale of the troops. [. . .] you. Won't you write them to inquire, "Why

are you doing this?" [. . .] peace(?) [. . . .] Does the king have(?) [. . .]? I swear
to God,[16] since I read the letters, I have not had [a moment's peace!]

===== **Fragment Mentioning a Prophet** =====

65. Lachich 16 (BM 125 706)
(589 B.C.E.)

A

[. . . .] חמן[. . . .]	1
[. . . .] ה הי[. . . .]	2
[. . . .]שׁלח / הע[. . . .]	3
[. . . .] בני . ס]פֿר . . .]	4
[. . . .] י]הו הנבא[. . .]	5
[. . . .]מ[. .]	6

B

[. . . . א][. . . . .]	7
[. . . .]ע[. . .]	8
[. . . .]שלח א[. . . .]	9
[. . . .]ד]בר וח[. . .]	10

[. . .] send the [. . . the] letter of the sons of [. . .][17] [. . .-ya]hu the prophet
[. . .] send [. . .] word and [. . .].

===== **Rations** =====

66. Lachish 5 (BM 125 703)
(589 B.C.E.)

ישמע]יהוה את אד[ני	1
]שמעת של]ם וטב]עת[	2

3 ‏[כים עת כי]ֹם מי . עבדך
4 ‏כלב . כי . [ש]לחתה אל עבד-
5 ‏ך ֹ א[ת] הֹ[ס]פרם כ]זא-
6 ‏[ת] ֹ השב . עבדך . הספר-
7 ‏ם . אל אדני . יראך י-
8 ‏הוה ֹ הקצר ֹ בטֹב
9 ‏הים . האל . עבדך . י‹ב›א
10 ‏טביהו . זרע למלך

May YHWH send you, my lord, the very best possible news this very day!
  I am nothing but a dog, why have you sent me these letters? I am returning them to you.
  I pray that YHWH will let you see a good harvest today. Is Tobyahu going to send me some of the king's grain?

67. Lachish 9 (BM 125 705)
(589 B.C.E.)

A

1 ‏ישמע יהוה ֹ את אד-
2 ‏ני ש[ן]מעת]שלם ו[טב]
3 ‏[וע]ת תן . לחם 10 ו-
4 ‏[יי]ן 2 השֹב
5 ‏[ל]עבדך ר-
6 ‏בר ב-

B

7 ‏יר שֹלֹמֹיהו . א-
8 ‏שר נעשה . מֹ-
9 ‏חר

May YHWH send you, my lord, the very best possible news.
Please issue ten loaves of bread and two jugs[18] of wine to bearer.
Send me word back by Shelemyah as to what we are to do tomorrow.

Notes

1. Perhaps "fresh troops," from Arad to reinforce some other post.
2. The translation follows the interpretation of Pardee (1978b: No. 17; 1982: 55).
3. One of the temple personnel (Levine 1969: 49–51).
4. The sense seems to be, "It is taken care of," or "I have dealt with it."
5. The reference to the temple is unprecedented in Hebrew inscriptions. Only the temple in Jerusalem can be meant. At an earlier time there was a small temple in Arad, but it had been destroyed before this letter was written.
6. Literally, "*baths*"; see the glossary. The total ration called for is around 120–135 liters (32–36 gallons).
7. Literally, "from what is left of the first flour." If this does mean the oldest, and if the Greeks themselves brought the note to Arad, it implies that they could not understand it. Whether the "wine from the craters" was also second-rate, we do not know. Wine could not be stored for any extended time is such large vessels. Perhaps the wine was watered in accordance with Greek taste (Pardee 1982: 32).
8. I have followed Pardee (1982: 35) in taking the literal sense to be "bind them up with dough." A less likely alternative yields "hurry them on, without letting up" (Lemaire mentions this possibility without accepting it [1977: 165]; cf. Smelik 1991: 109).
9. One *bath?*
10. Aharoni (1981: 32, 34) and Pardee (1982: 51–52) restore the place-name "Ziph." No word can be seen in the photograph, but Aharoni sees faint traces on the original.
11. Literally, "Who is your servant but a dog, that my lord should remember his servant?" See also Nos. 64 and 66 and 2 Kgs 8:13.
12. Literally, "As YHWH lives, if . . . ." In the highly emotional style of this letter, the conventional expression takes on a tone close to profanity.
13. The context implies that that letter was seized as subversive material. The text literally says only, "a letter of T."
14. Neither the pronunciation nor the location of this place is known.
15. Or, "just as you ordered."
16. Literally, "As YHWH your God lives."
17. Or, "my son's letter."
18. Probably "*baths*" is implied (Pardee 1982: 106; see the wine rations mentioned in Nos. 56–58).

VIII

Canaanite Letters
(Edomite, Ammonite, and Phoenician)

<hr/>

Introduction

Each of the three letters in this chapter is written in a different Canaanite dialect: *Edomite* (No. 68), the language of the indigenous inhabitants of southern Transjordan during the biblical period; *Ammonite* (No. 69), the language of north central Transjordan around modern Amman; and *Phoenician* (No. 70), the language of the seafaring Canaanites of the Lebanese coast and their colonies around the Mediterranean.

No other Edomite, Ammonite, or Phoenician letters have been found. They do, however, have some broad generic similarities with one another and with the Aramaic and Hebrew letters in this collection. Nothing of the ancient Ammonite language has survived aside from a handful of short inscriptions (most of them mere fragments) and a few seals, to which we may add a few place-names and personal names from the Bible and ancient Near Eastern epigraphic sources. The written remains of Edomite are even more sparse — a few barely decipherable ostraca, a number of seals, and some names. No. 68 is the only connected Edomite text of any sort known. Phoenician is much more extensively attested, but No. 70 is the only letter.

Written in similar scripts, Edomite and Ammonite appear to have differed from Hebrew mainly in matters of pronunciation and word formation. The finer points of difference are, of course, invisible behind the consonantal writing system. Phoenician diverged more greatly from these three, but probably not so greatly as to prevent mutual intelligibility.

The three Canaanite letters all relate to economic transactions, specifically to loans: the repayment of a loan of grain (No. 68), a pledge of grain (No. 69), and an overdue payment of a loan of silver (No. 70). Thousands of comparable economic texts are known in Akkadian.

117

No. 68 was found in 1983 at Horvat Uza in the eastern Negeb. The site is less than six miles south-southeast of Arad. Some scholars have suggested that it is to be identified with the site called Ramat-Negeb in a Hebrew letter from Arad (No. 53). While this is uncertain, Horvat Uza was definitely on the fringes of Judean territory. The letter is roughly contemporary with the Arad letters. Unlike the Arad corpus, the Edomite note gives no hint of border tensions of the time. No. 69, the Ammonite letter, was found at Tell el-Mazar in the central Jordan Valley (modern Jordan, near Deir Alla), and is also a recent discovery.

The Phoenician letter (No. 70), written on a poorly preserved papyrus found at Saqqara, Egypt, has been known since the early 1940s. Most Phoenician inscriptions have been discovered either in the Lebanese homeland or in the Punic settlements of North Africa, but there is scattered evidence for the presence of Phoenicians in various centers along the Nile in the sixth and fifth centuries as far south as Abu Simbel. As with some of the Aramaic letters (see the introduction to chapter 2), is it unclear whether the familiar terms of address ("my sister," etc.) imply real kinship.

═══════ An Edomite Note Concerning Grain Delivery ═══════

68. Horvat Uza Edomite O.
(Eastern Negev; late seventh-early sixth century B.C.E.)

1 אָמֹר . למלך . אמר . לבלבל.

2 השלם . את . והברכתך

3 לקום . ועת . תן . את . האכל

4 אשר . עמֹד . אחאמה [. . .]

5 והרם ען]אל . על מזֹנו. [. . .]

6 [. .] חמר . האכל

A message from Lumalak[1] to Bulbul.

Are you well? I bless you by Qaus.

Send the feed-grain which is owed to Ahamah [. . .], and have Uzziel deliver it to the granary: [. . .] *homers* of feed grain.

An Ammonite Note Concerning Grain

69. Tell El-Mazār Ammonite O. (Ost. No. 3, JUM 223/79)
(Tell El-Mazār, Jordan; 600–550 B.C.E.)

1 אמר פלט אמר לאחה לעבדא]ל[ן

2 שלם את ועת שע]ר[ת אתן

3 לך שערת לשבת . כער]בן[

4 ועֹת תֹן לפלט אן]חך[

5] . [ישב בא] . [

A message from Pelet to his brother Ebed-El.
Are you well?
I am sending you some barley to deposit as a pledge. Now give it to your
brother Pelet [. . .] who lives in [. . .].

A Phoenician Letter

70. Saqqara Phoenician Papyrus (Cairo, Eg. Mus.)
(late sixth century [?] B.C.E.)

A

1 . ושלם את . בשא . אחתך . אמר . ארשת . לאחתי . אמר
     אף אנך . שלם . ברכתך . לב-

2 . אפקן . שלם . יפעלך . תחפנחם . אל . ולכל . עלצפן
     הכספ . אש . שלחת . לי . ותנת-

3 על . ומלאת] . [ען אתכֹר . ל]. . .[ן . הן]ר[3 לי משנק]ל . [ן
     תפני. אית . כל כ-

4 . אש אדע]ן[ברר . בטח]אֹתֹי[. ויתת . בֹך . אש לי . סף
     במא]ן . . [ת וש-

5 לחת לי את ספר הנקת אש למין]. . [כי

B

6   אל ארשת בת אן שׁמ]נין תן[

To my sister, from your sister Basu.
   Are you well? I am.
   I bless you by Baal-Saphon and all the gods of Tahpanhes. May they keep
you well!
   I am still waiting for the money you sent me. Now you need to pay me
an additional   3   [. . .]. Then I can pay Tipni(?) all the money I have.[2] [. . .].
Send me the receipt which [. . .].

Address: To Arishut daughter of Eshmunyaton.

Notes

   1. Possibly a scribal error for "Elimelek" (Ruth 1:2, 3, etc.), or "Elmalak" (Vattioni
1970: No. 11).
   2. Or perhaps, "the entire debt which I owe."

Sources

Editions listed generally include translations, except for Rosenthal (Aramaic) and Davies (Hebrew). The sign # indicates the text number in editions conventionally cited in that manner; otherwise page numbers are indicated. Under "Translation" are added only important translations published without the original text. Partial translations are listed in only a few cases of special importance. For more extensive bibliography, see, on the Aramaic letters, Porten 1968; Grelot 1972; Gibson 1975; Porten and Yardeni 1986; and Fitzmyer and Kaufman 1992 (also Whitehead 1974 [for Nos. 37–48]); and, on the Hebrew and Phoenician texts, see Pardee 1982, with more recent additions in Smelik 1991.

1. **Editions:** Lidzbarski 1921: 5-15; Dupont-Sommer 1944-45: 24-61; Donner and Röllig 1962-68: #233; Gibson 1975: #20.
2. **Editions:** Dupont-Sommer 1948b: 43-68; Donner and Röllig 1962-68: #266; Fitzmyer 1965: 41-55; Gibson 1975: #21; Porten 1981: 36-52; Porten and Yardeni 1986: #1.1.
3. **Editions:** Bresciani-Kamil 1966: #1; Milik 1967: 581; Gibson 1975: #27.i; Porten and Yardeni 1986: #2.3.
   Translation: Grelot 1972: #25.
4. **Editions:** Bresciani-Kamil 1966: #3; Milik 1967: 582-83; Gibson 1975: #27.iii; Porten and Yardeni 1986: #2.4.
   Translation: Grelot 1972: #27.
5. **Editions:** Bresciani-Kamil 1966: #4; Milik 1967: 583; Gibson 1975: #27.iv; Porten and Yardeni 1986: #2.1.
   Translation: Grelot 1972: #28.
6. **Editions:** Bresciani-Kamil 1966: #2; Milik 1967: 581-82; Gibson 1975: #27.ii; Porten and Yardeni 1986: #2.2.
   Translation: Grelot 1972: #26.
7. **Editions:** Bresciani-Kamil 1966: #6; Milik 1967: 547-49; Gibson 1975: #27.vi; Porten and Yardeni 1986: #2.6.
   Translation: Grelot 1972: #30.

8. **Editions:** Bresciani-Kamil 1966: #5; Milik 1967: 583-84; Gibson 1975: #27.v; Porten and Yardeni 1986: #2.5.
   Translation: Grelot 1972: #29.
9. **Editions:** Bresciani-Kamil 1966: #7; Milik 1967: 584; Gibson 1975: #27.vii; Porten and Yardeni 1986: #2.7.
   Translation: Grelot 1972: #31.
10. **Editions:** Bresciani 1960: 11-24; Fitzmyer 1962: 15-22; Gibson 1975: #28; Porten and Yardeni 1986: #3.3
    Translation: Grelot 1972: #14.
11. **Editions:** Bresciani 1960: 11-24; Fitzmyer 1962:22-23; Porten and Yardeni 1986: #3.4.
12. **Editions:** *CIS* ii: #137; Sachau 1911: #78/3; Dupont-Sommer 1948a: 117-30; Levine 1964: 18-22; Donner and Röllig 1962-68: #270; Gibson 1975: #123.
    Translations: Porten 1968: 275; Grelot 1972: #21
13. **Editions:** Sayce 1909: 154-55; *RES* #1295; Lidzbarski 1909-15: 119-21.
    Translations: Porten 1968: 179; Grelot 1972: #92.
14. **Edition:** Dupont-Sommer 1963: 53-58.
    Translation: Grelot 1972: #99.
15. **Editions:** Sachau 1911: #76/1; Greenfield 1960: 98-102.
    Translations: Porten 1968: 87, 132; Grelot 1972: #95.
16. Same as No. 15.
17. **Edition:** Cowley 1929: 107-111.
    Translation: Grelot 1972: #23.
18. **Editions:** Sayce-Cowley 1906: "M"; Lidzbarski 1903-7: 236-38; *RES* #492, #1800; Lindenberger, "Slave-Girl"
    Translations: Porten 1968: 204; Grelot 1972: #22.
19. **Editions:** Sayce 1911: 183-84; *RES* #1793; Dupont-Sommer 1946-1947a: 46-51.
    Translations: Porten 1968: 131,276; Grelot 1972: #94.
20. **Editions:** Dupont-Sommer 1945: 17-28.
    Translations: Porten 1968: 275; Ginsberg 1969: 491; Grelot 1972: #87.
21. **Editions:** Aimé-Giron 1926: 27-29; Dupont-Sommer 1946-47b: 79-87.
    Translations: Porten 1968: 277; Grelot 1972: #90.
22. **Editions:** Dupont-Sommer 1949: 29-39; Rosenthal 1967: #II.A.5.
    Translation: Grelot 1972: #91.
23. **Edition:** Dupont-Sommer 1948a: 109-16.
    Translation: Porten 1968: 90, 277
24. **Edition:** Dupont-Sommer 1942-45: 65-75.
    Translations: Porten 1968: 276; Grelot 1972: #19.
25. **Edition:** Lozachmeur 1971: 81-93.

26. **Edition:** Dupont-Sommer 1957: 403-9.
27. **Editions:** Aimé Giron 1931: 6-7; Lidzbarski 1909-15: 121-22; *RES* #1296.
    Translation: Grelot 1972: #20.
28. Not previously published.
29. Not previously published.
30. **Editions:** Sachau 1911: #6; Cowley 1923: #21; Porten and Yardeni 1986: #4.1.
    Translation: Grelot 1972: #96.
31. **Editions:** Sachau 1911: #11; Cowley 1923: #38; Porten and Yardeni 1986: #4.3.
    Translation: Grelot 1972: #98.
32. **Editions:** Sachau 1911: ##43 + 33; Cowley 1923: ##56 + 34; Porten and Yardeni 1986: #4.4.
    Translation: Grelot 1972: #100.
33. **Editions:** Euting 1903: 297-311; Cowley 1923: #27; Porten and Yardeni 1986: #4.5.
    Translation: Grelot 1972: #101.
34. **Editions:** Sachau 1911: ##1-2; Cowley 1923: ##30-31; Rosenthal 1967: #II.A.1; Porten and Yardeni 1986: ##4.7-4.8.
    Translations: Ginsberg 1969: 491-92; Grelot 1972: #102.
35. **Editions:** Sachau 1911: #3; Cowley 1923: #32; Porten and Yardeni 1986: #4.9.
    Translations: Ginsberg 1969: 492; Grelot 1972: #103.
36. **Editions:** Sachau 1911: #5; Cowley 1923: #33; Porten and Yardeni 1986: #4.10.
    Translations: Ginsberg 1969: 492; Grelot 1972: #104.
37. **Editions:** Driver 1954, 1965: #2; Whitehead 1974: 38-42; Porten and Yardeni 1986: #6.4.
    Translation: Grelot 1972: #62.
38. **Editions:** Driver 1954, 1965: #4; Whitehead 1974: 48-53; Porten and Yardeni 1986: #6.8.
    Translation: Grelot 1972: #65.
39. **Editions:** Driver 1954, 1965: #3; Whitehead 1974: 42-48; Porten and Yardeni 1986: #6.3.
    Translation: Grelot 1972: #64.
40. **Editions:** Driver 1954, 1965: #5; Whitehead 1974: 53-59; Rosenthal 1967: #II.A.2; Porten and Yardeni 1986: #6.7.
    Translation: Grelot 1972: #66.
41. **Editions:** Driver 1954, 1965: #6; Whitehead 1974: 59-68; Porten and Yardeni 1986: #6.9.
    Translation: Grelot 1972: #67.
42. **Editions:** Driver 1954, 1965: #8; Rosenthal 1967: #II.A.3; Whitehead 1974: 77-84; Porten and Yardeni 1986: #6.11.

Translation: Grelot 1972: #69.
43. **Editions:** Driver 1954, 1965: #7; Whitehead 1974: 69-76; Porten and Yardeni 1986: #6.10
    Translation: Grelot 1972: #68.
44. **Editions:** Driver 1954, 1965: #10; Whitehead 1974: 90-94; Porten and Yardeni 1986: #6.13.
    Translation: Grelot 1972: #71.
45. **Editions:** Driver 1954, 1965: #11; Whitehead 1974: 94-99; Porten and Yardeni 1986: #6.14.
    Translation: Grelot 1972: #72.
46. **Editions:** Driver 1954, 1965: #9; Rosenthal 1967: #II.A.4; Whitehead 1974: 84-89; Porten and Yardeni 1986: #6.12.
    Translation: Grelot 1972: #70.
47. **Editions:** Driver 1954, 1965: #12; Whitehead 1974: 99-108; Porten and Yardeni 1986: #6.15.
    Translation: Grelot 1972: #73.
48. **Editions:** Driver 1954, 1965: #13; Whitehead 1974: 108-12; Porten and Yardeni 1986: #6.16.
    Translation: Grelot 1972: #74.
49. **Editions:** Sachau 1911: #8; Cowley 1923: #26; Porten and Yardeni 1986: #6.2.
    Translation: Grelot 1972: #61.
50. **Editions:** Naveh 1960; Gibson 1971: 26-30; Pardee 1982: #1; Davies 1991: #7.001.
    Translations: Albright 1969: 568; Lemaire 1977: 259-68.
51. **Editions:** Aharoni 1975; 1981: #40; Pardee 1982: #22; Davies 1991: #2.040.
    Translation: Lemaire 1977: 207-9.
52. **Editions:** Aharoni 1975; 1981: #88; Davies 1991: #2.088.
    Translation: Lemaire 1977: 220-21.
53. **Editions:** Aharoni 1975; 1981: #24; Pardee 1982: #20; Davies 1991: #2.024.
    Translation: Lemaire 1977: 188-95.
54. **Editions:** Aharoni 1975; 1981: #21; Pardee 1982: #19; Davies 1991: #2.021.
    Translation: Lemaire 1977: 186-87.
55. **Editions:** Aharoni 1975; 1981: #18; Pardee 1982: #18; Davies 1991: #2.018.
    Translation: Lemaire 1977: 179-84.
56. **Editions:** Aharoni 1975; 1981: #1; Pardee 1982: #2; Davies 1991: #2.001.
    Translation: Lemaire 1977: 155-61.
57. **Editions:** Aharoni 1975; 1981: #2; Pardee 1982: #3; Davies 1991: #2.002.

Translation: Lemaire 1977: 161-63.
58. **Editions:** Aharoni 1975; 1981: #3; Pardee 1982: #4; Davies 1991: #2.003.
Translation: Lemaire 1977: 163-66.
59. **Editions:** Aharoni 1975; 1981: #17; Pardee 1982: #17; Davies 1991: #2.017.
Translation: Lemaire 1977: 174-79.
60. **Editions:** Aharoni 1975; 1981: #16; Pardee 1982: #16; Davies 1991: #2.016.
Translation: Lemaire 1977: 172-74.
61. **Editions:** Torczyner 1938: #2; Diringer 1953: #2; Pardee 1982: #24; Davies 1991: #1.002.
Translations: Albright 1969: 322; Lemaire 1977: 97-100.
62. **Editions:** Torczyner 1938: #3; Diringer 1953: #3; Pardee 1982: #25; Cross 1985; Davies 1991: #1.003.
Translations: Albright 1969: 322; Lemaire 1977: 100-109.
63. **Editions:** Torczyner 1938: #4; Diringer 1953: #4; Pardee 1982: #26; Davies 1991: #1.004.
Translations: Albright 1969: 322; Lemaire 1977: 110-17.
64. **Editions:** Torczyner 1938: #6; Diringer 1953: #6; Pardee 1982: #28; Davies 1991: #1.006.
Translations: Albright 1969: 322; Lemaire 1977: 120-24.
65. **Editions:** Torczyner 1938: #16; Diringer 1953: #16; Pardee 1982: #33; Davies 1991: #1.016.
Translations: Albright 1969: 322; Lemaire 1977: 131.
66. **Editions:** Torczyner 1938: #5; Diringer 1953: #5; Pardee 1982: #27; Davies 1991: #1.005.
Translations: Albright 1969: 322; Lemaire 1977: 117-20.
67. **Editions:** Torczyner 1938: #9; Diringer 1953: #9; Pardee 1982: #30; Davies 1991: #1.009.
Translations: Albright 1969: 322; Lemaire 1977: 127-28.
68. **Edition:** Beit Arieh and Cresson 1985.
69. **Editions:** Yassine and Teixidor 1986; Aufrecht 1989: 334-37.
70. **Editions:** Aimé-Giron 1941; Donner and Röllig 1964-68: #50; Pardee 1982: 165-68.

Concordance of Texts*

This Volume	Conventional Designation	*TADA*	*DAE*
1	Ashur		
2	Adon	1.1	
3	Hermopolis 1	2.3	25
4	Hermopolis 3	2.4	27
5	Hermopolis 4	2.1	28
6	Hermopolis 2	2.2	26
7	Hermopolis 6	2.6	30
8	Hermopolis 5	2.5	29
9	Hermopolis 7	2.7	31
10	Padua 1	3.3	14
11	Padua 2	3.4	
12	*AAB* .47		21
13	*AAB* .30		92
14	*AAB* .33, #44		99
15	*AAB* .22(a)		95
16	*AAB* .22(b)		95
17	*AAB* .34		23
18	*AAB* .36		22
19	*AAB* .20		94
20	*AAB* .33, #70		87

* There are no standard designations for the Aramaic ostraca (Nos. 12–29). References are given to entries in *AAB* (Fitzmyer and Kaufman 1992: 102–13), where additional bibliography may be found. In *AAB*, references to the ostraca all begin with "B.3.c" followed by the numbers listed in the chart above.

This Volume	Conventional Designation	*TADA*	*DAE*
21	*AAB* .28		90
22	*AAB* .33, #152		91
23	*AAB* .33, #16		
24	*AAB* .33, #69		19
25	*AAB* .33, #228		
26	*AAB* .33, #186		
27	*RES* 1296		20
28	BM 45035(a)		
29	BM 45035(b)		
30	*AP* 21	4.1	96
31	*AP* 38	4.3	98
32	*AP* 5634	4.4	100
33	*AP* 27	4.5	101
34	*AP* 30/31	4.7/4.8	102
35	*AP* 32	4.9	103
36	*AP* 33	4.10	104
37	*AD* 2	6.4	62
38	*AD* 4	6.8	65
39	*AD* 3	6.3	64
40	*AD* 5	6.7	66
41	*AD* 6	6.9	67
42	*AD* 8	6.11	69
43	*AD* 7	6.10	68
44	*AD* 10	6.13	71
45	*AD* 11	6.14	72
46	*AD* 9	6.12	70
47	*AD* 12	6.15	73
48	*AD* 13	6.16	74
49	*AP* 26	6.2	61
50	Yavneh-Yam		
51	Arad 40		
52	Arad 88		
53	Arad 24		
54	Arad 21		
55	Arad 18		

This Volume	Conventional Designation	*TADA*	*DAE*
56	Arad 1		
57	Arad 2		
58	Arad 3		
59	Arad 17		
60	Arad 16		
61	Lachish 2		
62	Lachish 3		
63	Lachish 4		
64	Lachish 6		
65	Lachish 16		
66	Lachish 5		
67	Lachish 9		
68	Horvat Uza		
69	Tel el-Mazar		
70	Saqqara Phoen		

Bibliography

Académie des Inscriptions et Belles-Lettres
1889   *Corpus inscriptionum semiticarum.* Part 2, vol. 1. Paris: Imprimerie Nationale.
1900–68 *Répertoire d'épigraphie sémitique.* 8 vols. Paris: Imprimerie Nationale.
Aharoni, Yohanan
1975   *Arad Inscriptions* Jerusalem: Israel Exploration Society. [Modern Hebrew].
1981   *Arad Inscriptions.* Trans. by Judith Ben-Or. Ed. and rev. by Anson F. Rainey. Jerusalem: Israel Exploration Society.
[Aimé-]Giron, Noël
1926   "Trois ostraca araméens d'Éléphantine." *Annales du Service des Antiquités de l'Égypte* 26: 27–29.
1931   *Textes araméens d'Égypte.* Cairo: Service des Antiquités de l'Égypte.
1941   "Adversaria semitica (III): VIII, Baal Saphon et les dieux de Tahpanhès dans un nouveau papyrus phénicien." *Annales du Service des Antiquités de l'Égypte* 40: 433–60.
Albright, William F.
1969   "A Letter from the Time of Josiah." P. 586 in *Ancient Near Eastern Texts Relating to the Old Testament.* Ed. by J. B. Pritchard. Princeton: Princeton University Press.
Aufrecht, Walter E.
1989   *A Corpus of Ammonite Inscriptions.* Ancient Near Eastern Texts and Studies 4. Lewiston, NY/Queenston, Ont./Lampeter, Wales: Edwin Mellen.

129

Baly, Denis
   1984   "The Geography of Palestine and the Levant in Relation to Its
           History." Pp. 1–24 in *The Persian Period*. Ed. by W. D. Davies and
           Louis Finkelstein. *The Cambridge History of Judaism* 1. Cam-
           bridge: Cambridge University Press.

Beit-Arieh, Itzhaq, and Bruce Cresson
   1985   "An Edomite Ostracon from Horvat Uza." *Tel Aviv* 12: 96–101.

Benz, Frank L.
   1972   *Personal Names in the Phoenician and Punic Inscriptions*. Studia Pohl
           6. Rome: Biblical Institute Press.

Bivar, A. D. H.
   1985   "Achaemenid Coins, Weights and Measures." Pp. 610–39 in *The
           Median and Achaemenian Periods*. Ed. by Ilya Gershevitch. *The
           Cambridge History of Iran* 2. Cambridge: Cambridge University
           Press.

Boardman, John
   1988   "The Greek World." Pp. 95–178 in *Persia, Greece and the Western
           Mediterranean, C. 525–479 B.C.* [plates]. Ed. by John Boardman.
           The Cambridge Ancient History 4, suppl. Cambridge: Cambridge
           University Press.

Boardman, John, ed.
   1988   *The Cambridge Ancient History* 4, *Persia, Greece and the Western
           Mediterranean, C. 525–479 B.C.* Cambridge: Cambridge Univer-
           sity Press.
   1988   *The Cambridge Ancient History* 4, suppl. *Persia, Greece and the
           Western Mediterranean, C. 525–479 B.C.* [plates]. Cambridge:
           Cambridge University Press.

Brandenstein, Wilhelm, and Manfred Mayrhofer
   1964   *Handbuch des Altpersischen*. Wiesbaden: Harrassowitz.

Bresciani, Edda
   1960   "Papiri aramaici egiziani di epoca persiana presso il Museo
           Civico di Padova." *Revista degli studi orientali* 35: 11–24.
   1984   "The Diaspora: C. Egypt, Persian Satrapy." Pp. 358–72 in *The
           Persian Period*. Ed. by W. D. Davies and Louis Finkelstein. *The
           Cambridge History of Judaism* 1. Cambridge: Cambridge Univer-
           sity Press.
   1985   "The Persian Occupation of Egypt." Pp. 502–28 in *The Median
           and Achaemenian Periods*. Ed. by Ilya Gershevitch. *The Cambridge
           History of Iran* 2. Cambridge: Cambridge University Press.

Bresciani, Edda, and Murad Kamil
   1966   "Le lettere aramaiche di Hermopoli." Pp. 356–428 in *Atti della
           Accademia Nazionale dei Lincei*. Classe di Scienze morali, storiche
           e filologiche, ser. 8, no. 12. Rome: Accademia Nazionale dei
           Lincei.

Bright, John
1981   *A History of Israel.* Philadelphia: Westminster.
Burn, A. R.
1985   "Persia and the Greeks." Pp. 292–391 in *The Median and Achaemenian Periods.* Ed. by Ilya Gershevitch. *The Cambridge History of Iran* 2. Cambridge: Cambridge University Press.
Coats, George
1970   "Self Abasement and Insult Formulas." *JBL* 89: 14–26.
Cogan, Mordechai, and Hayim Tadmor
1988   *II Kings.* Anchor Bible 11. Garden City, NY: Doubleday.
Cook, J. M.
1983   *The Persian Empire.* London: J. M. Dent & Sons.
1985   "The Rise of the Achaemenids and Establishment of Their Empire." Pp. 200–91 in *The Median and Achaemenian Periods.* Ed. by Ilya Gershevitch. *The Cambridge History of Iran* 2. Cambridge: Cambridge University Press.
Cowley, A. E.
1923   *Aramaic Papyri of the Fifth Century B.C.* Oxford: Clarendon.
1929   "Two Aramaic Ostraka." *Journal of the Royal Asiatic Society* 107–12.
Cross, Frank Moore
1985   "A Literate Soldier: Lachish Letter III." Pp. 41–47 in *Biblical and Related Studies Presented to Samuel Iwry.* Ed. by Ann Kort and Scott Morschauser. Winona Lake, IN: Eisenbrauns.
Dalman, Gustaf H.
1938   *Aramäisch-Neuhebräisches Handwörterbuch zu Targum, Talmud und Midrasch.* Hildesheim: Olms.
Dandamaev, Muhammad A.
1984a   "The Diaspora: A. Babylonia in the Persian Age." Pp. 326–42 in *The Persian Period.* Ed. by W. D. Davies and Louis Finkelstein. *The Cambridge History of Judaism* 1. Cambridge: Cambridge University Press.
1984b   *Slavery in Babylonia: From Nabopolassar to Alexander the Great (626–331 BC).* Trans. by Victoria Powell. Ed. by Marvin A. Powell and David B. Weisberg. DeKalb, IL: Northern Illinois University Press.
Dandamaev, Muhammad A., and Vladimir G. Lukonin
1989   *The Culture and Social Institutions of Ancient Iran.* Ed. and trans. by Philip L. Kohl and D. J. Dadson. Cambridge: Cambridge University Press.
Davies, G. I.
1991   *Ancient Hebrew Inscriptions.* Assisted by M. N. A. Bockmuehl, D. R. de Lacey, and A. J. Poulter. Cambridge: Cambridge University Press.

Davies, W. D., and Louis Finkelstein, eds.
1984   *The Cambridge History of Judaism* 1, *The Persian Period.* Cambridge: Cambridge University Press.

Dever, William G.
1985   "Weights and Measures." Pp. 1126–31 in *Harper's Bible Dictionary.* Ed. by Paul J. Achtemeier et al. San Francisco: Harper & Row.

Dietrich, Manfried
1970   *Die Aramäer Sudbabyloniens in der Sargonidenzeit.* Alter Orient und Altes Testament 5/1. Neukirchen-Vluyn: Neukirchener Verlag; Kevelaer: Butzon & Bercker.

Diringer, David
1953   "Early Hebrew Inscriptions." Pp. 331–59 in *The Iron Age.* Ed. by Olga Tufnell *et al.* Lachish 3. London: Oxford University Press.

Donner, Herbert, and Wolfgang Röllig
1962–68 *Kanaanäische und Aramäische Inschriften.* 3 vols. Wiesbaden: Harrassowitz.

Driver, Godfrey R.
1954   *Aramaic Documents of the Fifth Century B.C.* Oxford: Clarendon.
1965   *Aramaic Documents of the Fifth Century B.C.* Rev. ed. Oxford: Clarendon.

Dupont-Sommer, A.
1942–45 "Un ostracon araméen inédit d'Éléphantine adressé à Ahutab." *Revue des études sémitiques* n.v.: 65–75.
1944–45 "L'ostracon araméen d'Assour." *Syria* 24: 24–61.
1945   "Le syncretisme religieux des juifs d'Éléphantine d'après un ostracon araméen inédit." *Revue de l'histoire des religions* 130: 17–28.
1946–47a "Sur la fête de la Pâque dans les documents araméens d'Éléphantine." *Revue des études juives* 107: 39–51.
1946–47b "Maison de Yahvé et vêtements sacrés à Éléphantine." *Journal asiatique* 235: 79–87.
1948a   "Ostraca araméens d'Éléphantine." *Annales du Service des Antiquités d'Égypte* 48: 109–30.
1948b   "Un papyrus araméen d'époque saïte découverte à Saqqarah." *Semitica* 1: 43–68.
1949   "L'ostracon araméen du sabbat." *Semitica* 2: 29–39.
1957   "Un ostracon araméen inédit d'Éléphantine." *Rivista degli studi orientali* 32: 403–9.
1963   "Un ostracon araméen inédit d'Éléphantine (collection Clermont-Ganneau N° 44)." Pp. 53–58 in *Hebrew and Semitic Studies Presented to Godfrey Rolles Driver.* Ed. by D. Winton Thomas and W. D. McHardy. Oxford: Clarendon.

Euting, J.
1903   "Notice sur un papyrus Égypto-araméen de la Bibliothèque

Impériale de Strasbourg." *Mémoires presentées par divers savants à l'Académie des Inscriptions et Belles-Lettres* 11: 297–311.

Fitzmyer, Joseph A.
1962   "The Padua Aramaic Papyrus Letters." *JNES* 21: 15–24.
1965   "The Aramaic Letter of King Adon to the Egyptian Pharaoh." *Biblica* 46: 41–55.
1981   "Aramaic Epistolography." *Semeia* 22: 25–56.

Fitzmyer, Joseph A., and Stephen Kaufman
1992   *An Aramaic Bibliography:* Vol. 1, *Old, Official, and Biblical Aramaic.* Baltimore/London: Johns Hopkins.

Frye, Richard N.
1984   *The History of Ancient Iran.* Handbuch der Altertumswissenschaft. Munich: C. H. Beck.

Gershevitch, Ilya, ed.
1985   *The Cambridge History of Iran 2, The Median and Achaemenian Periods.* Cambridge: Cambridge University Press.

Gibson, John C. L.
1971   *Textbook of Syrian Semitic Inscriptions:* Vol. 1, *Hebrew and Moabite Inscriptions.* Oxford: Clarendon.
1975   *Textbook of Syrian Semitic Inscriptions:* Vol. 2, *Aramaic Inscriptions.* Oxford: Clarendon.

Ginsberg, H. L.
1969   "Letters of the Jews of Elephantine." Pp. 491–92 in *Ancient Near Eastern Texts Relating to the Old Testament.* Ed. by J. B. Pritchard. Princeton: Princeton University Press.

Greenfield, Jonas C.
1960   "Le Bain des Brebis." *Orientalia* 29: 98–102.
1985   "Aramaic in the Achaemenian Empire." Pp. 698–713 in *The Median and Achaemenian Periods.* Ed. by Ilya Gershevitch. *The Cambridge History of Iran 2.* Cambridge: Cambridge University Press.

Grelot, Pierre
1972   *Documents araméens d'Egypte.* Littératures anciennes du proche-orient 5. Paris: Cerf.

Hallock, R. T.
1985   "The Evidence of the Persepolis Tablets." Pp. 588–609 in *The Median and Achaemenian Periods.* Ed. by Ilya Gershevitch. *The Cambridge History of Iran 2.* Cambridge: Cambridge University Press.

Hayes, John H., and James Maxwell Miller
1977   *Israelite and Judean History.* Philadelphia: Westminster.

Hillers, Delbert R.
1979   "Redemption in Letters 6 and 2 from Hermopolis." *Ugarit-Forschungen* 11: 379–82.

Hinz, Walther
1973   *Neue Wege im Altpersischen.* Göttinger Orientforschungen. Wiesbaden: Harrassowitz.

Hoffner, Harry A.
1990   *Hittite Myths.* SBL Writings from the Ancient World 2. Atlanta: Scholars Press.

Holladay, John S.
1976   "Of Sherds and Strata: Contributions Toward an Understanding of the Archaeology of the Divided Monarchy." Pp. 253–93 in *Magnalia Dei: The Mighty Acts of God.* Ed. by Frank Moore Cross, Werner Lemke, and Patrick D. Miller. Garden City, NY: Doubleday.

Jastrow, Marcus
1903   *A Dictionary of the Targumim, the Talmud Babli and Yerushalmi, and the Midrashic Literature.* New York: Jastrow.

Kaufman, Stephen A.
1974   *Akkadian Influences on Aramaic.* Oriental Institute Assyriological Studies 19. Chicago: University of Chicago Press.

Kent, R. G.
1953   *Old Persian: Grammar, Texts, Lexicon.* American Oriental Series 33. New Haven: American Oriental Society.

Kornfeld, Walter
1978   *Onomastica aramaica aus Ägypten.* Österreichische Akademie der Wissenschaften, Philosophisch-historische Klasse: Sitzungsberichte 333. Vienna: Österreichische Akademie der Wissenschaften.

Kraeling, Emil G.
1953   *The Brooklyn Museum Aramaic Papyri.* New Haven: Yale University Press.

Lemaire, André
1977   *Inscriptions hébraïques:* Vol. 1, *Les ostraca.* Littératures anciennes du proche-orient 9. Paris: Cerf.

Lemaire, André, and Jean-Marie Durand
1984   *Les inscriptions araméennes de Sfiré et l'Assyrie de Shamshi-Ilu.* École pratique des hautes études; IVe Section, Sciences historiques et philologiques. II Hautes études orientales, no. 20. Geneva/Paris: Droz.

Levine, Baruch A.
1964   "Notes on an Aramaic Dream Text from Egypt." *JAOS* 84: 18–22.
1969   "Notes on a Hebrew Ostracon from Arad." *IEJ* 19: 49–51.

Lidzbarski, Mark
1903–7   *Ephemeris für semitische Epigraphik,* vol. 2. Giessen: A. Töpelmann.
1909–15   *Ephemeris für semitische Epigraphik,* vol. 3. Giessen: A. Töpelmann.

1921   *Altaramäische Urkunden aus Assur. Ausgrabungen der Deutschen Orient-*
        Gesellschaft in Assur; E: Inschriften; V Altaramäische Urkunden.
        Leipzig: Hinrichs.
Lindenberger, James M.
1984   *The Aramaic Proverbs of Ahiqar.* Baltimore/London: Johns
        Hopkins University Press.
[. . .]   "A Slave-Girl at Elephantine: A New Reading of RES 492b."
        Maarav [forthcoming].
[. . .]   "Whatever Happened to Vidranga? A Jewish Liturgy of Cursing
        from Elephantine (*AP* 30:16–17a//31:15–16a)." [forthcoming].
Lozachmeur, Hélène
1971   "Un ostracon araméen inédit d'Éléphantine (Collection
        Clermont-Ganneau N° 228)." *Semitica* 21: 81–93.
Lyle, Evelyn
1966   *The Search for the Royal Road.* London: Vision.
Malamat, Abraham
1968   "The Last Kings of Judah and the Fall of Jerusalem." *IEJ* 18:
        137–56.
1974   "The Twilight of Judah: In the Egyptian-Babylonian Mael-
        strom." Vetus Testamentum Supplements 28: 123–45.
Mazar, A.
1981   "The Excavations at Khirbet Abu Et-Twein and the System of
        Iron Age Fortresses in Judah [Modern Hebrew]." *Eretz Israel* 15:
        229–49 [Eng. summary, pp. 83*–84*].
Milik, J. T.
1967   "Les papyrus araméens d'Hermopolis et les cultes syro-phéni-
        ciens en Égypte perse." *Biblica* 48: 546–628.
Miller, Patrick D.
1971   "The *Mrzh* Text." Pp. 37–54 in *The Claremont Ras Shamra Tablets.*
        Ed. by Loren R. Fisher. Analecta orientalia 48. Rome: Ponti-
        ficium Institutum Biblicum.
Moorey, P. R. S.
1988   "The Persian Empire." Pp. 1–94 in *Persia, Greece and the Western
        Mediterranean, C. 525–479 B.C.* [plates]. Ed. by John Boardman.
        The Cambridge Ancient History 4, suppl. Cambridge: Cambridge
        University Press.
Naveh, Joseph
1960   "A Hebrew Letter from the Seventh Century." *IEJ* 10: 129–39.
1962   'The Excavation at Mesad Hashavyahu: Preliminary Report."
        IEJ 12: 89–113.
1970   *The Development of the Aramaic Script.* Israel Academy of Sciences
        and Humanities, vol. 1, no. 1. Jerusalem: Israel Academy of
        Sciences and Humanities.

Oded, Bustenay
1977   "Judah and the Exile." Pp. 435–88 in *Israelite and Judean History.*
          Ed. by John H. Hayes and James Maxwell Miller. Philadelphia:
          Westminster.
1979   *Mass Deportations and Deportees in the Neo-Assyrian Empire.* Wies-
          baden: L. Reichert.
Olmstead, A. T.
1948   *History of the Persian Empire.* Chicago: University of Chicago
          Press.
Oppenheim, A. L.
1985   "The Babylonian Evidence of Achaemenian Rule in Mesopo-
          tamia." Pp. 529–87 in *The Median and Achaemenian Periods.* Ed. by
          Ilya Gershevitch. *The Cambridge History of Iran* 2. Cambridge:
          Cambridge University Press.
1977   *Ancient Mesopotamia: Portrait of a Dead Civilization.* Rev. by Erica
          Reiner. Chicago: University of Chicago Press.
Pardee, Dennis
1978a   "The Judicial Plea from Mesad Hashavyahu (Yavneh-Yam): A
          New Philological Study." *Maarav* 1: 33–66.
1978b   "Letters from Tel Arad." *Ugarit-Forschungen* 10: 289–336.
1982   *Handbook of Ancient Hebrew Letters.* Collaborators S. David
          Sperling, J. David Whitehead, and Paul E. Dion. SBL Sources
          for Biblical Study 15. Chico, CA: Scholars Press.
Porada, Edith
1985   "Classic Achaemenian Architecture and Sculpture." Pp. 793–827
          in *The Median and Achaemenian Periods.* Ed. by Ilya Gershevitch.
          The Cambridge History of Iran 2. Cambridge: Cambridge Univer-
          sity Press.
Porten, Bezalel
1968   *Archives from Elephantine: The Life of an Ancient Jewish Military
          Colony.* Berkeley/Los Angeles: University of California.
1979   "Aramaic Papyri and Parchments: A New Look." *BA* 42: 74–
          104.
1980   "Aramaic Letters: A Study in Papyrological Reconstruction."
          Journal of the American Research Center in Egypt 17: 39–75.
1981   "The Identity of King Adon." *BA* 44: 36–52.
1984   "The Diaspora: D. The Jews in Egypt." Pp. 372–400 in *The
          Persian Period.* Ed. by W. D. Davies and Louis Finkelstein. *The
          Cambridge History of Judaism* 1. Cambridge: Cambridge Univer-
          sity Press.
Porten, Bezalel, and Jonas C. Greenfield
1974   *Jews of Elephantine and Arameans of Syene: Aramaic Texts with Trans-
          lations.* Jerusalem: Academon.

Porten, Bezalel, and Ada Yardeni
1986   *Textbook of Aramaic Documents from Ancient Egypt: 1 Letters.* The Hebrew University Department of the History of the Jewish People, Texts and Studies for Students. Winona Lake, IN: Eisenbrauns.
1989   *Textbook of Aramaic Documents from Ancient Egypt: 2 Contracts.* The Hebrew University Department of the History of the Jewish People, Texts and Studies for Students. Winona Lake, IN: Eisenbrauns.

Price, M. Jessop
1988   "Coinage." Pp. 237–48 in *Persia, Greece and the Western Mediterranean, C. 525–479 B.C.* [plates]. Ed. by John Boardman. *The Cambridge Ancient History* 4, suppl. Cambridge: Cambridge University Press.

Pritchard, J. B., ed.
1969   *Ancient Near Eastern Texts Relating to the Old Testament.* Princeton: Princeton University Press.

Ridgway, David
1988   "Italy." Pp. 202–36 in *Persia, Greece and the Western Mediterranean, C. 525–479 B.C.* [plates]. Ed. by John Boardman. *The Cambridge Ancient History* 4, suppl. Cambridge: Cambridge University Press.

Rosenthal, Franz
1961   *A Grammar of Biblical Aramaic.* Porta linguarum orientalium, n.s. 5. Wiesbaden: Harrassowitz.

Rosenthal, Franz, ed.
1967   *An Aramaic Handbook.* 2 vols. Porta linguarum orientalium, n.s. 10. Wiesbaden: Harrassowitz.

Sachau, Edouard
1911   *Aramäische Papyrus und Ostraka aus einer jüdischen Militärkolonie zu Elephantine.* 2 vols. Leipzig: Hinrichs.

Saggs, H. W. F.
1984   *The Might That Was Assyria.* London: Sidgwick & Jackson.

Sayce, A. H.
1909–11 "An Aramaic Ostracon from Elephantine." Parts 1, 2. *Proceedings of the Society of Biblical Archaeology* 31: 154–55; 33: 183–84.

Sayce, A. H., and A. E. Cowley
1906   *Aramaic Papyri Discovered at Assuan.* London: A. Moring.

Segal, J. B.
1983   *Aramaic Texts from North Saqqâra.* Excavations at North Saqqâra: Documentary Series 4. London: Egypt Exploration Society.

Smelik, Klaas A. D.
1991   *Writings from Ancient Israel: A Handbook of Historical and Religious Documents.* Louisville: Westminster/John Knox.

Smith, Morton
1971   *Palestinian Parties and Politics That Shaped the Old Testament.* New York/London: Columbia University Press.
1984   "Jewish Religious Life in the Persian Period." Pp. 219–78 in *The Persian Period.* Ed. by W. D. Davies and Louis Finkelstein. *The Cambridge History of Judaism* 1. Cambridge: Cambridge University Press.
Sokoloff, Michael
1990   *A Dictionary of Jewish Palestinian Aramaic.* Ramat Gan: Bar Ilan University Press.
Stark, Jürgen Kurt
1971   *Personal Names in Palmyrene Inscriptions.* Oxford: Clarendon.
Torczyner [Tur-Sinai], Harry
1938   *The Lachish Letters.* Lachish 1. London: Oxford University Press.
Vattioni, F.
1970   "Epigraphia aramaica." *Augustinianum* 10: 493–532.
Vincent, Albert
1937   *La religion des judéo-araméens d'Éléphantine.* Paris: Paul Geuthner.
Von Soden, Wolfram
1965–81 *Akkadisches Handwörterbuch.* 3 vols. Wiesbaden: Harrassowitz.
Wente, Edward
1990   *Letters from Ancient Egypt.* SBL Writings from the Ancient World 1. Atlanta: Scholars Press.
Whitehead, J. David
1974   "Early Aramaic Epistolography: The Arsames Correspondence." Ph.D. dissertation, University of Chicago.
1978   "Some Distinctive Features of the Language of the Aramaic Arsames Correspondence." *JNES* 37: 119–40.
Wilson, R. J. A.
1988   "The Western Greeks." Pp. 179–201 in *Persia, Greece and the Western Mediterranean, C. 525–479 B.C.* [plates]. Ed. by John Boardman. *The Cambridge Ancient History* 4, suppl. Cambridge: Cambridge University Press.
Wiseman, D. J.
1956   *Chronicles of Chaldean Kings, 626–556, in the British Museum.* London: British Museum.
1958   *The Vassal-Treaties of Esarhaddon.* London: British School of Archaeology in Iraq.
Yadin, Yigael
1984   "The Lachish Letters—Originals or Copies and Drafts?" Pp. 179–86 in *Recent Archaeology in the Land of Israel.* Ed. by Hershel Shanks. Washington: Biblical Archaeology Society.

Yassine, Khair, and Javier Teixidor
1986   "Ammonite and Aramaic Inscriptions from Tell El-Mazar in
        Jordan." *Bulletin of the American Schools of Oriental Research* 264
        (November): 45–50.
Yeivin, S.
1962   "The Judicial Petition from Mezad Hashavyahu." *Bibliotheca
        orientalis* 19: 3–10.

Glossary

ardab. A measure of capacity used in Egypt, approximately thirty liters (twenty-seven dry quarts). The size of a farm can be indicated by giving the number of *ardabs* of seed sown in it.

bath. A liquid measure roughly equivalent to twenty-two liters (5.5 liquid gallons), or about twice that amount, according to some.

Baal-Saphon (Baal Zephon). An ancient Canaanite high god, worshiped in Syria from the mid-second millennium. He was also known among the Semites in northern Egypt, where a town was named for him (Exod 14:2, 9).

Banit. Epithet of a divinity worshiped at Syene. Banit has been uncertainly identified with the Babylonian goddess Zarpanitu, consort of Marduk and mother of Nabu.

Beel-Shemayn (Baal Shamayim). "The Lord of Heaven," high god widely venerated among the Aramean and Canaanite peoples of Syria and northern Mesopotamia. Some reckoned him as chief of the pantheon.

Bes. A minor Egyptian god, often associated with children and childbirth. Bes is depicted as a grotesque dwarf with bow legs, a jug head, and a tail.

Bethel. Epithet of a west Semitic divinity worshiped in Syria-Palestine; literally "the house of God," or "the house of the god El." Bethel had a temple at Syene, and many Aramean personal names from Egypt are compounded with the name.

cubit. A unit of linear measure used in Egypt, Mesopotamia, and Israel. This measure was based on the distance from the elbow to the tip of the middle finger; there was no universal standard length. Measuring sticks found in Egypt indicate a long cubit (sometimes called "royal") of about

52.5 centimeters (20.6 inches), and a shorter cubit of approximately 45 centimeters (18 inches). There were long and short cubits also in Israel.

homer. A large measure of dry capacity used particularly for grain. Originally a donkey-load, the *homer* may never have been precisely defined, although most modern scholars estimate it between 134 and 209 liters (3.8 and 5 bushels).

Ishtar. Mesopotamian goddess of fertility and war. Her chief shrine was in Arbela.

karsh. The official standard of weight for silver in the Persian empire, the *karsh* weighed slightly less than ten Egyptian shekels. An extra *zuz* (half-shekel) was often added to the *karsh* to bring it up to ten-shekel weight, hence the conversion formula "one *zuz* to the ten," in economic documents of the period (Porten 1968: 66-67, 305-7).

Khnum. The Egyptian ram-god, guardian of the First Cataract of the Nile. His main temple was on the island of Elephantine, not far from the Jewish temple of YHW.

Marheshwan. The eighth month of the Babylonian-Jewish calendar, equivalent to October-November in the Julian calendar.

marzeah. Apparently a voluntary society which celebrated festal banquets in honor of the dead. There is scattered evidence for such associations in inscriptions from different parts of the ancient Near East from the fourteenth century B.C.E. down to the third century C.E., including the Hebrew Bible (Amos 6:7; Jer 16:5) and rabbinic sources (*Sipre* Num. 131; *Midr. Lev. Rab.* 5:3; *b. Mo'ed Qat.* 28b; *b. Ketub.* 8b, 69ab; *y. Ber.* 2:6a, top). See Porten 1968: 179-86; and Miller 1971.

Mehir. The sixth month in the Egyptian calendar, corresponding to Siwan, third month in the Babylonian-Jewish calendar (May-June).

mina. A medium unit of weight, equal to sixty shekels.

Nisan. First month in the Babylonian-Jewish calendar (March-April).

Nabu. Babylonian god, son of Marduk and Zarpanitu. Nabu was especially prominent in the late neo-Babylonian period.

Ptah. Egyptian creator god, whose primary place of worship was Memphis.

qab. A measure of capacity equivalent to slightly over one liter (about one dry quart).

Qaus (Qos). The national divinity of ancient Edom.

Queen of Heaven. A high goddess who had a temple in Syene. The epithet refers to the ancient Canaanite goddess of love and warfare known variously as Anath, Asherah, and Astarte, or possibly her Babylonian counterpart, Ishtar. According to Jer 7:18; 44:17-19, 25, the Queen of Heaven was venerated by Judean refugees fleeing to Upper Egypt in Jeremiah's time.

shekel. A unit of weight calculated at Elephantine as 8.76 grams (.31 ounce). Some shekel weights from monarchic Israel weigh around 11.4 grams, and there was also a "heavy" shekel weighing nearly twice as much as the Elephantine shekel.

talent. A large unit of weight, equal to 360 shekels.

Tammuz. Fourth month in the Babylonian-Jewish calendar, named for the dying and rising vegetation god (June-July).

Tebeth. Tenth month in the Babylonian-Jewish calendar (December-January).

YHH, YHW, YHWH. Variant forms of the consonants forming the name of the God of Israel. The first two forms appear in Aramaic texts from Egypt; the third is the usual Hebrew form.

zuz. A half-shekel.

Indexes

Gender cannot always be determined, but names clearly identifiable as feminine are so indicated.

I. Deities

Baal-Saphon, 120
Banit [f.], 7, 25, 27, 28, 30
Beel-shemayn, 21
Bes, 73
Bethel, 25, 29

Ishtar [f.], 73

Khnum, 45, 59, 63, 66, 70

Nabu, 7, 25, 26

Ptah, 7, 25, 26, 28, 29, 30, 31, 32

Qaus (Qos), 118
Queen of Heaven, 25, 29

YHH, 37, 45, 49
YHW, 7, 25, 34, 59, 63, 66, 67, 69, 70
YHWH, 7, 8, 54, 106, 110, 111, 113, 115, 116

II. Personal Names

Language and regional abbreviations: Akk = Akkadian, Anat = Anatolian, Arab = Arabic, Can = Canaanite, Ed = Edomite, Eg = Egyptian, Gk = Greek, Pers = Persian, Phoen = Phoenician. Names with no indication are Hebrew, Aramaic, or generic northwest Semitic (or are names generally known from ancient history). It is not always possible to distinguish between Akkadian and west Semitic names, and frequently impossible to distinguish between Aramaic, Hebrew and Canaanite. Bib. indicates conventional spelling in English versions of the Bible. Egyptian and Persian names commonly cited in Greek form are indicated as follows: Achaemenes (Pers > Gk).

Abbaya (Akk), 17, 20
Achaemenes (Pers > Gk), 25, 72
Adon (Can), 9, 10, 11, 17, 18, 21, 100
Ahamah (Ed), 118
Ahat-sin (Akk?), 27
Ahatubasti (Akk? or Can-Eg compound; var. Hatubasti), 86
Ahhapi (Eg), 75, 77, 78, 89

Ahishay (vocalization?; Akk?), 20
Ahiyahu, 112
Ahutab [f.], 40, 41, 44, 47, 48
Ahyo (= Bib. Ahijah), 44, 61
Akba, 28
Alpay (> NT Gk Alphaeus), 48
Ami (vocalization?), 24, 33
Ammuwana (Anat), 79

143

III. Places

IV. Subjects

abuse, 72

accountants, 82, 85, 87, 92, 94

adjutant, 20

administration (*see also* Persian administration), 3, 25, 71, 73

administrative districts (*see also* satrapy, province), 25

administrative documents, 72, 73

Akkadian language and texts (*see also* Assyrian, Babylonian), 1, 2, 4, 7, 10, 15, 117

altar, 67, 68

alternative name-forms, 24

ambiguity, 24

Ammonite inscriptions, 117

Ammonite language, 1, 117

Ammonites, 100

anger, 27

anointing, 67

appeal, 82

appointment, 72

Arameans, 1, 2, 16, 100

ardab (*see* glossary), 41, 69, 82

aristocracy (*see also* nobles), 73

army (*see also* Assyrian army, Babylonian army, Egyptian army, Persian army, officers, military, soldiers, etc.), 16, 105

arrest (*see also* imprisonment, prisoners), 24, 53, 55, 59, 60, 79, 113

arsenic, 93, 94

art and artists, 4, 73, 102

artisans, 73, 81, 83, 87

Assyria, 73

Assyrian army (*see also* army), 102

Assyrian art, 4

Assyrian kings (*see also* kings), 17, 20

Assyrians, 16, 36, 51

Assyrian soldiers (*see also* army), 16, 99

Assyrian texts, 15

asylum, 101

auxiliary troops (*see also* army), 18, 21

babies and children, 33, 39, 44

Babylonian army (*see also* army), 99, 100, 102

Babylonian Chronicle, 17, 99, 100

Babylonian invasion, 2, 9, 101, 102

Babylonian nationalists, 16

Babylonians (*see also* Chaldeans), 99

Babylonian texts (*see also* Babylonian chronicle), 7, 72

Babylonian tribes, 17

barley (*see also* grain), 28, 46, 50, 69, 119

basins, 67

basket, 47

beans (*see also* vegetables), 47

beating, 89

beer, 80

Behistun inscription, 25

Bit-Amukkani (tribe; *see* index of place names)

blessing(s), 7, 8, 25, 26, 28, 29, 30, 31, 32, 34, 45, 49, 54, 57, 58, 59, 61, 66, 103, 106, 110, 118, 120

boat-building materials, 92

boatmen (*see also* ferryman), 37, 92

boat(s), 31, 46, 52, 73, 92, 94, 95

boatwright, 92, 94

bookkeepers, 35

border tensions, 118

bow, 95

bran, 51

branding (*see* slave-mark)

brazier, 63

bread, 40, 41, 42, 44, 101, 107, 108, 116

bribes, 55, 56, 63, 70

bronze, 67, 93

bureaucracy, 3, 73

burning, 17, 20, 55

burnt offering (*see also* offering, sacrifices), 67, 69

Canaanite languages, 117

Canaanite letters, 3, 6, 8, 9

Canaanites, 117

fasting, 55, 67
feed-grain (*see also* grain), 118
fermented drink (*see also* beer, wine), 58
ferryman (*see also* boatmen), 48
fetters, 21
fever, 39
field hand(s), 10
financial records, 72
fingerbreadths, 93
fire, 16, 20
first drafts, 53, 55
fish, 49
fittings, 63, 67
flour (*see also* grinding), 41, 42, 44, 48, 80, 101, 107, 116
fodder, 81
food (*see also* various foodstuffs), 100
food-warden, 94
fortress (*see also* citadel), 55, 63, 66, 67, 68, 69, 79, 92, 100, 101, 102
fragmentary letter(s), 9, 15, 17, 24, 53, 54, 56, 71, 101
fugitives, 20, 21

garda (*see* household staff)
garment(s) (*see also* clothing, dress, tunic), 10, 23, 24, 28, 35, 37, 45, 96, 97
garrison, 57, 58, 63, 79, 101
gate, gateway, 61, 67, 102
goat, 42, 69
gods, 21, 54, 57, 58, 61, 67, 90, 120
gold, 67, 73
goldsmiths, 73
goods, 23, 61, 63, 71
governor(s), 21, 55, 63, 66, 68, 96
grain (*see also* barley, wheat, meal offering), 30, 89, 101, 115, 117
granary, 118
grant, 75
grazing lands, 72
Greek papyri, 3
Greeks, 25, 101, 107, 108, 109, 116
Greek sources, 72
Greek wars, 25

greeting formulas, 6
grinding, 19, 40, 44
guarantor, 27
gunwale, 93, 94
guts, 67

handbreadths, 93
harvest, 97, 102, 115
harvesters, 97
hearing (legal), 55, 63
Hieratic, 100
high priest (*see also* priests), 67
highway, 73
hoeing, 47
homer (*see* glossary; *see also* donkey-load), 107, 118
honorific family language, 7, 24, 118
horse, 87
horseman (*see also* equestrian), 73, 87
household staff (*garda*), 72, 95

Imperial Aramaic, 2, 10
imprisonment (*see also* arrest, prisoners, release), 3, 20, 24, 40, 55, 61, 72, 79
incense (*see also* offering), 55, 67, 68, 69
incompetence, 72
inscriptions (*see also* Ammonite inscriptions, Assyrian texts, Babylonian texts, Phoenician inscriptions, cuneiform texts), 1, 10, 101
instability, 25, 53
insubordination, 72, 76, 103
insurrection, rebellion, etc., 16, 19, 25, 26, 72, 79, 82, 83
intelligence (military), 3, 101, 102
intercalary month, 38
interest, 36, 85
interrogation, 17
inventory, 42, 52, 108
investigators, 63
I.O.U., 24
iron, 93
irony, 103

Jewish soldiers (*see also* army), 57, 58
Jews, 53, 54, 55, 60, 67, 74

V. Biblical, Rabbinic, and Early Christian Literature